http://www.amazon.com

For detailed information about this and other orders, please visit
Your Account. You can also print invoices, change your e–mail
address and payment settings, alter your communication
preferences, and much more – 24 hours a day – at
http://www.amazon.com/your–account.

Returns Are Easy!

Visit http://www.amazon.com/returns to return any item –
including gifts – in unopened or original condition within 30
days for a full refund (other restrictions apply). Please have
your order ID ready.

Item Price	Total
$35.96	$35.96

	$35.96
ıg	$15.48
	$51.44
	$51.44
	$0.00

**Thanks for shopping at Amazon.com, and please
come again!**

 **amazon**.com.

 **amazon**.com. Amazon.com
1850 Mercer Rd.
Lexington, KY 40511

Billing Address:
Jim Carroll
7 Merriam Way
Upton, MA 01568
United States

Jim Carroll
7 Merriam Way
Upton, MA 01568
United States

Shipping Address:
Jim Carroll
7 Merriam Way
Upton, MA 01568
United States

1PS

fgdh35374/-1-/3596/next/1994960/508-320-0705

Your order of April 12, 2004 (Order ID 102-8498563-8891327)

Qty.	Item
	IN THIS SHIPMENT
1	**Software Product Management: Managing Software Development from Idea to Product to Marketing to Sales** Conde, Daniel --- Paperback (** P-1-I16D95 **) 1587622025

Subtotal
Shipping & Handli
Order Total
Paid via Amex
Balance due

This shipment completes your order.

ASPATORE
C-Level Business Intelligence™

Praise for Books, Briefs, Journals & Guides:

"By the time the industry is thinking about what the world thinks the technology leaders are thinking about, the truly influential are thinking about something else. Want to know what the real leaders are thinking about now? It's in here." - Dr. Carl Ledbetter, Novell, CTO

"An unprecedented collection of best practices and insight..." - Mike Toma, CTO, eLabor

"What C-Level executives read to keep their edge and make pivotal business decisions. Timeless classics for indispensable knowledge." - Richard Costello, Manager-Corporate Marketing Communication, General Electric (NYSE: GE)

"True insight from the doers in the industry, as opposed to the critics on the sideline." - Steve Hanson, CEO, On Semiconductor (NASDAQ: ONNN)

"Unlike any other business books, Inside the Minds captures the essence, the deep-down thinking processes, of people who make things happen." - Martin Cooper, CEO, Arraycomm

"A wealth of real world experience from the acknowledged industry leaders you can use in your own business." - Doug Cavit, CTO, McAfee.com

"Real advice from real experts that improves your game immediately." - Dan Woods, CTO, Capital Thinking

ASPATORE

C-Level Business Intelligence™

www.Aspatore.com

Aspatore publishes only the biggest names in the business world, including C-Level leaders (CEO, CTO, CFO, COO, CMO, Partner) from over half the world's 500 largest companies and other leading executives. By focusing on publishing only C-Level executives, Aspatore provides professionals of all levels with proven business intelligence from industry insiders, rather than relying on the knowledge of unknown authors and analysts. Aspatore publishes a highly innovative line of business intelligence publications including Inside the Minds, Bigwig Briefs, ExecRecs, Business Travel Bible (BTB), Brainstormers, The Business Reference Collection, The C-Level Test, Personal Intelligence Assistant (PIA) and Aspatore Business Reviews, in addition to other best selling business books, journals and briefs. Aspatore focuses on publishing traditional print publications with individuals, while our portfolio companies, Corporate Publishing Group (B2B agent & publisher) and ExecEnablers (business intelligence stores) focus on developing areas within the business and book publishing worlds. Aspatore is committed to providing our readers, authors, bookstores, distributors and customers with the highest quality books, journals, briefs and publishing execution available anywhere in the world.

SOFTWARE PRODUCT MANAGEMENT

Managing Software Development From Idea to Product to Marketing to Sales

Dan Condon

ASPATORE
C-Level Business Intelligence™

Published by Aspatore Books, Inc.
For corrections, company/title updates, comments or any other inquiries please email info@aspatore.com.

First Printing, 2002
10 9 8 7 6 5 4 3 2 1

ISBN 1-58762-202-5

Library of Congress Card Number: 2002108913

Edited by Jo Alice Hughes, Proofread by Ginger Conlon, Cover design by Kara Yates & Ian Mazie

Material in this book is for educational purposes only. This book is sold with the understanding that neither any of the authors or the publisher is engaged in rendering legal, accounting, investment, or any other professional service.

This book is printed on acid free paper.

A special thanks to all the individuals that made this book possible.

Special thanks to Ted Juliano

The views expressed by the individuals in this book do not necessarily reflect the views shared by the companies they are employed by (or the companies mentioned in this book). The companies referenced may not be the same company that the individual works for since the publishing of this book.

The views expressed by the endorsements on the inside of this book for the *Inside the Minds* series do not necessarily reflect the views shared by the companies they are employed by. The companies referenced may not be the same company that the individual works for since the publishing of this book.

SOFTWARE PRODUCT MANAGEMENT

Table of Contents

FORWARD

What This Book Is

This book is intended for software producers who want to make their products' stakeholders understand each other's needs, with the indirect goal of helping people work together better – an ambitious goal, but achievable. A secondary goal is to consider how to manage a product in a period of increased commoditization of some software technology products. Those two goals are not necessarily independent, since rapidly adapting a product to the needs of the key stakeholders – the end-users – is critical for ensuring differentiation.

The book deals primarily with enterprise software – products you sell to corporations, often through a direct sales force. I touch lightly on issues related to retail, or packaged software and the gray area in between, where some packaged software may be sold via your direct sales forces when enterprises need them in large volumes. But I feel this categorization is simple enough to promote the understanding of the distinctions and challenges for each type of product.

As you are aware, numerous books and articles have been written about techniques and processes for product management. I won't get into comparisons of them here. Different techniques are appropriate for different product development styles, and not one style is appropriate for all organizations.

Many of the issues discussed in *Software Product Management* seem to be common sense, lessons that can easily be applied to managing products other than software. Why discuss them if they're not unique to software? Because these issues arise often in software product management or have an inordinate influence in the development of software products. The problem of schedule slips, for example, tends to be particularly common in software, so we discuss it here, although our suggestions can be applied to almost any other product – chain saws, stereos, dog food – that has experienced delayed release problems.

Another topic we discuss is the issue of different stakeholders. People often neglect the role a product manager plays in coordinating the resources and efforts of multiple, varied groups with needs that often seem to conflict with each other.

In a dream world, everyone pulls together toward a common goal with little friction; great products get shipped on time; and every stakeholder is happy. In reality, even in well-oiled, high-functioning teams, we rarely see that happen. People bicker over seemingly small things; they point fingers; product managers get stressed out. I think what often happens is that individuals or groups do not understand the motivations of each stakeholder, what each team member has to offer, and how best to coordinate the efforts of all the team members. This book will provide some answers to these common problems.

Another dilemma we'll address is the conflicts that arise when a stakeholder makes decisions that are absolutely rational and correct for the assumptions and information available – but the assumptions and information available when the decision is made may be incorrect or incomplete or outdated. Who hasn't had to deal with that issue?

But this is not just a "people skills" book. I attempt to combine those goals with concrete things you can do to succeed in software product management. The book may be read by a variety of people – people who are product managers, those who aspire to be project managers, people who need to deal with product managers, or people who run companies.

Rather than give you specific, detailed instructions for doing your job, which varies from company to company, I concentrate on people you need to deal with, common misconceptions these stakeholders have of each other, and how to work together more effectively.

The goal of a product manager is defined here as managing a product from concept to release. I discuss whatever can be done in terms of dealing with people to help you reach that goal.

At the end, I provide context in the form of a brief history of the computing and software industry to illustrate how some of the lessons discussed earlier in the book can be used in adapting to the changes we see happening in the industry.

What This Book Is Not

I offer no in-depth details on what to do, step-by-step – this is a brief book of ideas, hints, and observations. If you want spreadsheet templates, survey forms, and samples of product requirements documents and marketing requirements documents, then you need to find other books. I recommend a few sources at the end of this book.

Software Product Management is not about project management – there are good books on that topic, too. By project management, I refer to the issues of resource allocation, scheduling tasks and dependencies, and managing the "traffic" of resources (such as engineers' allocated time). It's half art and half science, and it is sometimes assisted by project management tools. Other tools are related, such as requirements management tools. I believe requirements management is more closely related to understanding end-user needs, so we will touch on that topic here, as well.

This book is not about marketing and promotions. Although that is critical, it is only one facet of product management. Some aspects are closely tied to the product, but others are purely promotional and are better served in a discussion of marketing communication, which we don't provide here.

We do hope you find the book useful and enlightening.

Dan Condon
California, USA

EXECUTIVE SUMMARY

In this book I present my ideas on what defines software product management and what distinguishes it from other forms of product management. We concentrate on product management for enterprise software, commonly sold via direct sales forces. When you interact with various stakeholders, who range from engineering, sales, and support to marketing and finance, it's critical to understand the internal motivations that drive each group, and to recognize when those motivations may run counter to your overall product objectives or corporate goals.

Enterprise software falls into two basic categories – software that helps generate revenue and software perceived as internal efficiency tools. Salespeople often notice that revenue-generating software can gather many sponsors, but efficiency tools require a careful sales process where ROI is viewed as crucial.

A key role of sensible product management is to carefully set the goals that multiple parties all agree to and work toward. Since a product manager simply cannot keep tabs on all aspects of product development, setting clear, crisp, and unambiguous goals is crucial to making the development process efficient.

Good general management principles dictate good product management. But a few things do stand out. Building trust with different groups is critical. Unlike traditional management, where a manager may have some firsthand experience in performing the team members' tasks, a software product manager simply cannot be expected to have the depth of knowledge needed to understand each aspect in detail. Once you have assembled a good team, it is imperative to trust each person and avoid an unnecessary amount of second-guessing and micromanagement.

There are software tools and methodologies for assisting product management, but in general it's more important to return to basic principles and not get distracted with trendy processes. Yet, some tools do assist with the complex task of the bookkeeping of the requirements-gathering process.

The latter part of *Software Product Management* explores a variety of helpful hints for avoiding common misconceptions. We finish with a look toward the future, where increasing commoditization of software and hardware systems threatens to change many basic assumptions that lead to product design and development, as well as the marketing and sales processes.

Although we like to think of the technology evolution as a clean line of progression, I believe a set of accidental occurrences in the past 20 years has laid the groundwork for increased commoditization of software. This is yet another step in the overall technical trend of lowering costs and standardized technologies. But I believe the combination of the rise of highly portable, grassroots-driven systems software and infrastructure software (such as Java, J2EE, and open-source systems, such as Linux), combined with commodity hardware (made possible by Intel and Microsoft) will threaten to change the revenue models of the software we create and sell today. This means product management and requirements-gathering become even more important in an age in which rapid changes occur.

WHAT IS PRODUCT MANAGEMENT, ANYHOW?

Product management means different things to different people. It's typical in Silicon Valley to have a product manager who wears multiple hats:

Product marketing: Writing collateral and white papers, dealing with sales issues, providing support, talking to analysts (often called outbound product management).
Product management: Defining product requirements, interfacing with engineering (often called inbound product management).

One person does both tasks in many startups. There's some logic to giving one person these responsibilities. The combination provides a manager with broad perspective; additionally, having one person lead both areas is efficient and reduces the chances of misunderstanding or miscommunication of the priorities required to shepherd the product.

If you have multiple product managers, carve up responsibilities horizontally, as opposed to placing people into functional silos. Give each product manager responsibility for some aspect of inbound management, as well as some aspect of outbound management. This arrangement encourages the development of a broader perspective among product managers. As a company gets larger, it is inevitable for people to get placed into more functional positions (i.e., 100 percent inbound or outbound).

Other companies have different job categories. Microsoft, for example, has a program manager category that differs from a standard product manager category. A program manager is a technical person who worries about everything – through the release of a product. The distinction is simple: Program managers deal with the "stuff" in the box – the software and the documentation. (Of course, downloaded software does not have a box, but you get the idea.) Product marketing deals with the marketing of the box. So program management tasks include:

❑ Design
❑ Obtaining requirements

- ❏ Writing specs
- ❏ Implementation
- ❏ Coding coordination (Program managers do not write the code, but, with engineering managers, they coordinate the efforts to track release schedules and bug fixes.)
- ❏ Documentation management (user education)
- ❏ Betas
- ❏ Finding and coordinating a Beta test release
- ❏ Releasing the product
- ❏ Creating the final deliverable sent to manufacturing

Program management is a broadly defined job, and some program managers will concentrate on certain aspects over others. Nevertheless, a Microsoft program manager is often quite different from other companies' program managers, who are concerned more with project management and resource allocation.

At Microsoft there is usually a separate product manager. This is often generally referred to as product marketing (which leads to confusion in outsiders who are not familiar with the nomenclature). This position deals with:

❏ Promotions and ad campaigns
❏ Sales channel issues
❏ Dealing with press and analysts
❏ Getting product manufactured and distributed

It's almost the same split between outbound and inbound product management I mentioned earlier. In general, I think the technical job requirements of a Microsoft program manager are deeper than that of a *typical* inbound product manager.

There is also a separate *marketing* group at Microsoft that does cross-product marketing tasks – that is, marketing tasks that span multiple product group boundaries. This may include vertical marketing, creating an indirect sales channel, and divisionwide advertising campaigns.

It is often very confusing, since the term *product management* means different things to different firms.

At companies such as Oracle, the definition of a product manager may more closely resemble that of Microsoft's program manager. An Oracle product marketing manager may perform the job of the Microsoft product manager.

Emphasis of This Book

Given the different definitions of the term *product manager*, you may wonder what this book will emphasize. Will it be product management in the technical, inbound sense, or product management with an outbound emphasis? Or will it be both?

I will concentrate on *product*-related issues, as opposed to marketing and promotion. But I'll still touch lightly on marketing issues when the topic is relevant.

WHAT'S DIFFERENT ABOUT SOFTWARE?

What's different about software, compared to selling PCs or other high-tech products – or even standard products, such as housewares, cosmetics, or cars? Don't they all have product (some call them brand) managers?

Differences in Details

The differences lie in a number of details:

- ❑ Software is still not a mature product area. The market needs, the demand levels, and the technology basis are still rapidly changing. You cannot market software in a "steady" state. It's true that cosmetics and cars undergo rapid innovation, too, but not on the level that software experiences.

- ❑ The software business has different driving factors. It doesn't cost much to manufacture software, so you don't need to worry much about managing the efficiencies of the supply chain or controlling manufacturing costs. You need not worry about whether to outsource or manufacture in-house. Margins may be extremely high, especially if you OEM the product. On the other hand, the research and development costs are still very high, and for many companies there is the risk of launching a product into an uncharted market, with a fair amount of guess work involved in predicting true requirements.

❑ Software is perceived to be "just bits" that can be changed at any time, so companies may start to lose discipline with the product release process. This perception is inaccurate. Although you do not need to put as much effort into a new release as, say, retooling a metal stamping plant or reconfiguring an automobile assembly line, neither can you simply send out patches or make changes to the released product mid-stream, without making a formal re-release. In reality, many aspects of a product release cannot be waved away by a magic wand just because software is a "set of bits," as opposed to a large chunk of iron.

Packaged Versus Direct Sales Software

Software comes in many forms. It may be:

❑ A desk productivity tool, which is radically different from an enterprise business program

❑ A graphic design tool, which differs from a database or information management tool

❑ A game or entertainment product, as opposed to something meant to encourage productivity

❑ A product sold to be installed on an end-user's computer, as opposed to a service delivered over a network (sometimes called software for rent)

Rather than deal with these distinctions separately, we split the types into two broad, black-and-white categories:

1. Packaged software, the type we find on a software or office supply store shelf, sold at a set price

2. Direct sales software, whose price and support terms clients may need to negotiate with the sales reps who will call on them

There are, of course, shades of gray in between. For example, a VAR (value-add reseller) can buy packaged software, customize it, and sell a combined package. But this somewhat simple two-part distinction allows us to capture many of the defining characteristics; whereas, the product management approaches require a different way of thinking. These two large buckets allow me to combine:

❑ Software that requires close, constant interaction with the end-user, through continual adjustments

❑ Software that requires intense preplanning and infrequent ability to make changes

Applications Elsewhere

Certainly today we have many variations that may not fall cleanly into one of these two categories.

Games, for example, were traditionally sold as consumer retail products. Joe Consumer purchased a CD-ROM (or a ROM cartridge); he inserted it into to his home computer or game console; and there were no changes to the product until a new version came out. Now there are online gaming communities, where the software effectively resides on the Net and is rented to Joe by the month. Even traditional games have updates and patches he can download.

Enabling technologies make these changes possible. Application services are offered on the Web by ASPs (application service providers). This trend may accelerate via the adoption of Web services (.NET, XML-based, etc.).

Can you use this information to manage internal software projects within your IT shop? For the most part, the answer is yes.

Commonalities: Your internal customers are customers in every traditional sense of the word. They just happen to work for the same company you work for. They praise you, and they complain; they may fund your group; and they require support. They sound like customers to me!

Differences: Certainly, you know your customers intimately; they are not an abstract notion gathered through market research or via requirements funneled through a sales group. The myriad of support and post-sales issues are radically different from those surrounding a retail product, because the standard marketing issues or release issues may not be relevant.

Yet I believe there are enough similarities among all software products, and my simple taxonomy allows the discussion to move forward. You only need to figure out where in the spectrum your system resides and apply the right lessons for your needs.

SOFTWARE PRODUCT TYPES

Following are some general characteristics of direct sales and packaged software. If you are not sure where your product resides, use this discussion as a refresher.

Direct Sales Enterprise Software

Direct customer sales: Your client deals with your company or its partners directly. Lots of "high touch" is involved. For smaller customers, your company's inside sales group (i.e., telephone sales) may handle their sales needs or may meet them through a reseller (VAR or systems integrator). For large or key customers, your company may send a sales rep with a systems engineer (someone who is technical and knows the product in detail) to handle their pre- and post-sales needs and may assign a technical account manager for post-sales needs.

Negotiation: Prices are often negotiated, and product configuration is often complex. Support (or maintenance) contracts are often negotiated in the initial sales contract. Your enterprise customer rarely sees a complete price list for enterprise-class software. If the software is sold through reseller channels, they may see a published price list, but you still need to negotiate the service needed to install and maintain the software. In general, many line items are negotiated, and a price list, if published, is rarely the final word in your client's calculation of their final outlay.

Relatively low volume: You often sell in the hundreds, or perhaps a few thousand packages. You charge relatively high prices per unit, and there is an annuity revenue stream based on maintenance or support contracts (see below).

Support costs and maintenance: This type of software typically is sold with a support contract (around 15 percent to 20 percent of the software price, paid annually).

Packaged or Retail Software

High volume: You hope to sell hundreds of thousands of units. The great financial benefit is that your product scales cleanly, since you do not need to build a very large pre-sales, consulting, or service organization to sustain a larger volume of sales. Once you pay the fixed cost of creating the software, the more you make, the more you profit. There isn't a lot of consulting that goes along with these sales. Usually, a customer support center is the only variable cost.

Lower price than enterprise software: Customers can put your software on their credit cards if they want. It can cost from $20 up to several thousand dollars. Typically, expensive software requires services to install and support. In our rather simplistic view, we will categorize expensive software as direct sales software. It's not always technically true, but it's usually the reality.

Indirect sales: You rarely sell this software directly to the customer. You sell it to a reseller (such as a store or a systems integrator). This has some implications for your connection with the customer, since you rarely know who bought your software, unless they registered their purchase by sending back a registration card or registering online (which happens rarely).

Open-Source Infrastructure Software

As I mentioned before, other models and categories for software exist that we won't list here. But I'll provide one example of something different – open-source infrastructure software. I treat this separately, since it is becoming an increasingly important software category.

Open-source software is usually low-cost, and it is not uncommon to see this software used in a business-critical area, such a Web server. So by price alone it fits into the "retail" bucket, but for practical reasons it is in the enterprise bucket.

Often, such software is made available in several tiers – free or low-cost editions for trials and simple deployments, and a more expensive tier for true business use. So in this case I will depart from using the price filter alone and categorize this software as enterprise or business software because of the ultimate use of the product. We'll touch on this type of software lightly as our discussion moves on.

Implications for Product Development

These distinctions make a big difference for your staff, largely in the issue of flexibility versus process. The main distinctions can be summarized as:

❏ Packaged software with firm shipping schedules
❏ Enterprise software with no rigid shipment dates

This distinction, again, sounds rather simplistic, but many aspects end up being distilled into these two characteristics. Let's illustrate this with an analogy.

Releasing Packaged Software

Releasing packaged software is almost like releasing a movie or a toy. You announce the shipment date, and you get people ready for the event, particularly in your sales channels – people who place the product in catalogs or announce its availability on Web site advertisements – teaser announcements that get people ready and create a buzz, promotions, upgrade mailings that deal with your existing customers.

So you are compelled to ship on time. The ship date becomes an immovable goal around which all activities orbit. In reality ship dates do slip, but in the grand scheme of things the ship date is the most sacred goal, and people march to meet that commitment.

The movie industry often works like that. If you have a Christmas release, you'd better finish on time or risk the loss of massive seasonal box office sales. The same goes for toys. You sell a lot at Christmas, and not much after that, since kids don't want a new toy in January. In either case, if you don't meet your ship date you risk losing a significant amount of your annual revenue stream.

The results: Your staff members get stressed out over the schedule. Features of your product may get slashed arbitrarily to make the ship date.

Having a seemingly arbitrary schedule is actually a blessing in disguise, since it forces all other decisions to support that goal. Some people who may be more concerned about the product, as opposed to the financial aspects, may think, "Wow, it does seem arbitrary – it's just a date. Why must we sacrifice the product to meet a date?"

Their analogy may be: If the stew takes longer to cook than expected, do you still serve it at 7 p.m., as promised, even if the beef is still raw and the vegetables are still crunchy? The wait staff are coming in to pick it up for their hungry customers. What do you do?

Having some fixed criteria is a good way to get disciplined. Going back to the analogy, the result is that you do not serve the stew in a raw state. Since you know ahead of time that the dinner is served at 7 p.m., you ensure, through adequate pre-planning, that the stew is ready by 7 p.m.

A well-defined goal makes all elements fall into place. When there is too much flexibility – too many degrees of freedom – the product can start to slip. Keeping the well-defined goal "sacred" reduces the risks of loss associated with schedule slips.

Releasing Enterprise Software

Having no rigid ship date is a mixed blessing. You get flexibility, but at what price?

Enterprise software tends to fall into the category of "no rigid ship date." Certainly, large software producers do make product announcements and are held more strictly to a ship date, but smaller enterprise software firms are known to be very flexible in their release dates.

You can slip without a huge penalty, since you don't need to coordinate a big set of "machinery" around a firm goal of the ship date. You don't have to cancel an upgrade promotion; you may not have a very large customer base; and you may be able to manage expectations through your sales force.

To return to our stew analogy, you get to cook the stew until it is done. You can taste-test it along the way. You want to add a little salt, and realize you added too much, so you add a little water to dilute it, but now you realize the stew is sort of watery and lacks character. You need to cook it more and add other ingredients. Now it's 9 p.m., and weren't the guests supposed to be eating around 8? They look awfully hungry now. You apologize. They're not very accommodating, but you'll manage, since this is your private dinner party (read: few enterprise customers), and not a huge banquet (read: large numbers of retail customers).

Since there is no obvious penalty, there is greater incentive for people to create reasons to slip, and reasons tend to creep in.

A sales executive may say, "Let's add one more *critical* feature for *my* customer, and then we can ship."

Support may say, "Please fix this bug, and then we can ship. If we don't fix it, our support costs will continue to be high."

PR may say, "Ship later, and we can announce at this show, where we have a great opportunity to be in the limelight! Other firms will be quiet, since they already made their announcements months ago."

Once you slip, as a result of any of these stakeholders' suggestions, the defining characteristic is a new ship date. You held out for more features and fewer bugs, but are you sure you accomplished that? Let's follow this story a little further.

Another sales executive may come back and say, "My customer requested this, so if you add one more feature, we can ship."

Quality assurance says, "Thanks to the changes and new features, you introduced 100 new bugs!" (And note that some of these bugs were introduced as a result of fixing some of the bugs the support group asked you to fix!)

Engineering says, "We've been in ready-to-ship mode for the past year, and we are all exhausted. We were supposed to start planning the next version, but since our resources have all been redirected to making this release, we can't plan for the next version."

Meanwhile, customers are not buying; they are waiting for the next version. Finance starts to float some bad sales projections to the CEO. Heads start to roll, and fingers start to point to someone else to blame.

Few Companies Are 100 Percent Either Way

Few companies are purely one way or the other in the direct versus packaged spectrum. You need to apply these lessons carefully. Stating with religious zeal that your product resides completely in one direction is a sure way to paint yourself into a corner. You need to examine your company's overall strategic goals and compare them with your decision-making process.

Our illustrative story may be extreme, with a rather unhappy ending. But its lesson is clear: Explore the needs of each individual stakeholder group, and consider their requirements so you can best understand how to address their needs when you make product decisions. You must understand your stakeholders so you can:

❏ Understand each group's motivations and incentives that make them behave in a certain way

❏ Learn each group's "hot buttons" – how to talk to each group in ways that are most appreciated about the issues that matter most to them

The behavior of each group of stakeholders is often similar regardless of the software product being created. An engineer, for example, enjoys writing good, stable code whether it is for a million customers or for a few hundred. But it's important to know the subtle differences where it matters.

In later chapters we'll examine some examples of behavior different stakeholders may reveal when they encounter situations that arise in the creation of different types of products.

ROI: A DIFFERENT

PERCEPTION OF SOFTWARE

Although the majority of the discussion in this book addresses software in terms of packaged and direct sales categories, there is another distinction worth considering as well.

Revenue Contributor or Cost Center?

The way a product is perceived...

❏ As a business tool that enables the generation of increased revenue for the customer's business (revenue contributors), or

❏ As an internal utility or tool that costs money and may streamline IT operations (cost centers)

...will affect not only the set of requirements for the product, but also ultimately the design. This is a somewhat obscure categorization, perhaps best explained through an example.

A customer relationship management (CRM) product often is considered to increase profits, since it enables the firm to handle customer contact more efficiently. The implication is that you get higher levels of satisfaction and sell more of the product or service.

Another example is the sales management aspect of sales automation tools. These tools enable people to track sales leads more effectively, so they are obviously sales-centered tools. E-commerce applications, which enable a company to deal with sales to customers, for example, are also good profit-centered products.

You can argue that these tools streamline operations. That's true, but the key difference is that these products are needed by operational business units, as opposed to IT, as we discuss next.

Examples of products considered to be cost-centers are tools used to assist internal people in making their operations more efficient, such as maintenance tools to assist the operations of an IT data center. They are all definitely useful products – they are just as useful as a sales-related tool – but the key difference is the perception. Motivations to fund these programs are actually quite different.

The distinction is often quite subtle, but it seems that products are often placed into one bucket or another when customers budget for them, and this has wide-ranging implications.

Market Perceptions: Cost Center Tool

If you have someone in marketing with plans to expand sales in their company, they would be more than happy to create and fund a product that can assist in sales. These entities become sponsors within the company who advocate purchasing the product. These business unit entities often have access to a wide range of funds to purchase your software product. So even though you may be selling the revenue-creating product to a group that is managed, deployed, or supported within IT, they can easily get budget from the marketing department to justify better sales support and better sales operations.

On the other hand, if you sell a cost-center tool, such as a utility used to monitor the performance of a database, the sales process and perceptions are radically different.

A natural question is, "Will I immediately make more money if I use this utility? The answer is "yes," in the long-term, but there are extra degrees of separation between IT effectiveness and revenue generation.

It is obviously difficult for a vendor's sales rep to talk to the customer's marketing department and ask, "Can you spend more money to purchase this database product because it will help you do your work better?" The answer is typically no, since it's hard to make the immediate connection. So IT utilities are often purchased out of general IT budgets that are often fixed, and they cannot be funded out of special business unit budgets.

Using the database utility example again, we can examine how the potential customer justifies the purchase.

The people in the database management group have to justify the cost of the product based on the return on investment within their budget. They have to determine whether it will save them more money than it costs to buy the product. With the budget used to manage their database (not for software and hardware, but for employee salaries, consultant fees, and expenses incurred through maintaining a database), they could justify the purchase by deferring additional hiring because this tool would make them more efficient, so they wouldn't have to hire as many people.

As simple as this may sound, it's difficult to sell using a pure return on investment strategy. ROI is a critical method for selling many types of software, but it needs to be clearly articulated, backed up with real data, and prepared to answer any "Show me!" questions. Revenue-based software products may be sold at a higher, conceptual level, and if a business unit sponsor feels it will benefit them, you can make a sale to fund a trial. Cost-centered tools are sold on a more cut-and-dried basis – using clear evidence of their cost savings.

Implications for Management and Design

What does this mean for product management and product design? You have to make sure the motivation for purchasing a product becomes much more obvious in:

❏ The enumeration of its feature set
❏ The requirements
❏ The way you position the product

If you have a product designed with ROI in mind as a primary justification, then either ROI-related tools need to be built into the product, or the methods for calculating the ROI need to be obvious in your marketing material.

You will need to offer an ROI calculator (effectively a spreadsheet) that you can either mail to people or have on a Web site. ROI-based sales marketed on a "trust me" attitude will not work. The buyers always want to enter their own data into the calculations to make sure the ROI applies to them.

But even if those things are accepted and considered sufficiently useful to ensure an initial pilot installation, to gain final acceptance, make all parties in the customer understand its needs, and finally purchase the product, you need to quantify the product's benefits.

To justify the existence of the product, we need to enable the customer to measure the ROI. This may be based on true operational data, as opposed to the hypothetical data entered in the ROI calculator.

True data enables people to understand how effective their purchase decisions are. If they were correct in the assumption that the product adds value, then the product will finally exit the pilot stage and get purchased. In the future the customer can add more licenses of the software through expansion to different departments or systems.

For example, with a tool that monitors the database performance, you may need to assure people that you can:

❏ Calculate and measure how database maintenance operations cost money before deploying the tool
❏ Measure the efficiency of the operations after you use the tool

You could determine the down time or the amount of time spent by IT staff performing manual database maintenance beforehand or the downtime incurred due to the lack of automated monitoring. Then you can measure the same time after deploying the tool. You could measure:

❏ Reduced downtime
❏ Increased the performance of the database
❏ Additional hardware purchases deferred because an old piece of hardware was still effective and efficient

These very direct comparisons are especially helpful in selling to IT organizations with lean budgets. Not only do these tools boost IT managers' effectiveness, but more important, the IT managers can use these tools to make themselves look better to their own managers

IT managers' budgets are under scrutiny from the CTO. If you can help justify the purchase of this software so that it helps them in the next budget cycle, you make their jobs easier, and that will make it easier to sell additional units.

Sales Generation Tool

We've just seen that ROI justification is very important for a cost-centered tool, and specific features in a *product* to measure ROI will help enable sales. You can use a similar tactic to justify software that increases sales, but this is often more difficult to do.

The results, such as increased sales, are figures you can't measure within your software product, since they are something you indirectly enable. Unlike the database tool example, you cannot measure transactions per second or throughput.

Fortunately, if you can measure tangible results, such as sales, it's possible to simply point to the increased sales (if they do indeed occur) or improved customer satisfaction as proof that your software is doing its job.

It can be difficult to trace the results directly back to your software, since so many other factors influence the result. But it's possible to measure other forms of effectiveness, provided the measurements are available on a before-and-after basis. The numbers can be gathered *after* your software is deployed, but it may be difficult to gather information from *before,* especially if tasks are performed manually.

Examples of CRM software for sales automation:

❑ Increase the number of leads handled (if it's a sales lead management product) in a call center, per unit of time, or on a per-person basis or

❑ Increase efficiency with the right leads sent to the right people the first time because the software enables improved targeting

Potential Pitfalls

There are some pitfalls in using ROI as justification because there are so many different ways people view ROI. ROI methodologies differ among companies. If you place a simple ROI calculator on your Web site, it may be viewed as overly simplistic, since it may not present things in a way the company is willing to value.

Some people use internal rate of return, while some people use measurements such as the payoff period. Others may consider net present value a proper way to measure ROI. Fortunately, these items can be converted to others, so you can find a way customize the results according to how a customer wants to view the world. But it is not always that easy.

ROI is also viewed with skepticism, since many companies show ROI values in a strange arms race–like manner. For instance, a company touts how their product can top someone else's ROI.

All too often the ROI calculator on a Web site shows stupendous ROI – returns of 1,000 percent are not unheard of. Of course, ridiculous results reduce credibility, and customers become jaded. You can dream of, but really cannot believe in, a product that claims it justifies your cost of the software in a matter of days or weeks.

Stating your benefits in realistically framed and pragmatic ways is best. On the cost side of the ROI calculation, include all the costs that are involved in deploying, training on, and installing the software. In practice, returns on many software products take a reasonable amount of time to realize, and in all honesty, in most cases you can't actually see payoffs immediately. But I think customers will appreciate your candor in this regard.

Another problem is that some of the payoffs aren't very obvious. Head-count efficiency is easy to calculate: "Product X can defer your expense of hiring additional IT people through increased efficiencies by automating tasks A, B, and C."

Opportunity cost-based calculations are more difficult. What is the cost of downtime? Some ads claim that if your business experiences some downtime on the system, even for a minute, it *can* cost $2 million or $3 million. How do they know? I suspect businesses do not shut down during the downtime, as people are resourceful and may fall back to manual methods. Of course, there is some cost, but people often make simplistic downtime calculations and pretend that all business comes to a halt. I believe those calculations are not genuine. It's easy to make some tenuous connection that is ultimately flawed. For example:

"My network is down, so my customers can't access data. My salespeople can't access information to enable them to do a sales call. I can't read my e-mail because my e-mail system is not available; therefore, I failed to contact my client in a timely way, and I've lost a potential sale."

As silly as this example may be, people are known for making such claims in their ROI descriptions.

To do a realistic ROI calculation, you need to spend a fair amount of time. Sales and sale consultants need to consult with the customer's IT organization and business managers to run a through analysis. But in reality, most people are quite busy, and it's very difficult for people to spend the time to find out what the customer-specific ROI criteria are. It's advisable, however, to at least have a framework ready so you can provide it if a customer requests it.

STAKEHOLDERS IN

DIRECT SALES SOFTWARE

Let's look at the stakeholders and see how they behave in each type of company, starting with direct sales software production.

Engineering

This group actually writes the software programs. We will also include the Quality Assurance, or QA, group in this category, although they have slightly different motivations. We will illustrate some potential conflicts between engineering and sales using several stories and examples. One example shows how short-term requests may be perceived, and how engineering may react to them. The other shows how rapid feedback using collaboration may help close the gap between customer requirements and engineering deliverables. Throughout, we'll make some generalizations about our groups, although we're fully aware that there are always exceptions.

The reason I illustrate engineering issues in the context of direct sales or enterprise software with examples of rapid requests and response to customer requirements is that rapid feedback is often a hallmark of direct sales software. As you are aware, it's not a "shot and forgot" style of product development. There's always plenty of feedback from the field, and effectively addressing those needs provides a great way to increase the chances of success in the marketplace. In general it's the problem of the "requirements/deliverable gap."

Short-term Requests and Prototypes

Let's consider how engineers react to rapid requests from customers, which are common in many enterprises. Requests are likely to come in at the last minute from customers during the beta testing process. Feature requests are relayed directly to the engineering groups, not filtered through market research, because a customer does have a direct voice – through your sales reps. The sales group's issue becomes, "If we add this feature, we can close the sale." That's reality, and that's how an enterprise software firm makes money.

Engineers may not react to this mode very well, and in particular, lots of engineers are resentful of last-minute requests. Why?

Engineers have an inherent desire for more predictable schedules and requests. It's not a form of laziness – it's often driven by a lack of resources and the need to maximize the resources they have. Engineers love being efficient – they are rational and logical, so they want to plan ahead. They are creating an architecture with a particular goal in mind, and basically, a change in plan may mean a change in design.

Related to this is a desire to design a general architecture. Engineers have a vision of a product, and the software program is often perceived to be a tightly crafted piece of machinery whose parts all work together well. Last-minute requests often disturb this tight design.

Engineers seek to be efficient in the way they code: They perceive systems with small, fast, tight code as a thing of beauty. Sloppy, monolithic code held together with bailing wire is an object of disgust. If time is available, sloppy code must be thrown away, or at least rewritten. That's because a lot of people treat their code as a piece of art. Engineers put tremendous care in their work; they take great pride in what they do. There is a fair amount of peer review and admiration for a well done piece of work.

Last-minute requests are often perceived to be extra "bags" that are thrown on the side of the program, which makes a program feel jury-rigged. So in an intuitive way, engineers resist such requests.

Many engineers want to work on the next cool thing, so once a product is ready to ship, engineers look forward to the next release, where they can put in new features and use or exploit new technologies. End-user requests may often (but not necessarily) require reworking old code, which is not as desirable as working on the "next big thing."

Lots of engineers are highly competitive with other engineers, and at the same time very cooperative, an apparent paradox. They take pride in creating something cool that others admire, and they also work closely with others in a team. They hate to let others down. If they are late in finishing a module they promised, they will work hard and late to get it done. Their effort stems from a strong code of ethics.

Now we need to answer this question: *How do you balance your need to increase revenues by being highly reactive to the market against your engineers' desire to carefully craft a work of art?*

I don't think these needs are mutually exclusive. Some of this conflict stems from the different time horizons perceived by the engineer group and the sales group. The sales group, because of the incentives they have, thinks in very short-term goals. Engineers tend to be longer-term focused. Engineers are, of course, aware of short-term revenue goals, but in general, goals for creating great works of engineering tend to be highly aligned with long-term goals. In other words, creating a quick-and-dirty piece of code is generally considered hack behavior.

One approach to resolving these differences is to set the right level expectations. Let's consider the issue of having a customer float an idea for product enhancement through the sales organization. The idea is somewhat half-baked, and there are many ambiguous parts to the requirement. The question is whether the idea is conveyed to the engineering organization as a solid request.

If you let it be known that this is a final requirement, then some engineers will start crafting good, solid code to meet those requirements. (Some pragmatic or cynical ones may wait a while.)

If you pull the rug out from under them later on with, "Oops, I didn't know...so we no longer need that feature," that hurts an engineer's feelings.

The code may get archived, but as far as the final product is concerned, the engineers' work of art is shoved aside as an unwanted experiment. "What an insult!" your engineers would say. An experienced engineer may treat it more pragmatically, acting as a professional about it and brushing it off, but I speculate that it hurts inside.

My recommendations are: If the requirements are not known clearly, let that be known. Create some prototypes, and let the prototype be field-tested by the customer who originally requested it.

As long as engineering knows they're creating potentially throw-away code, then they will not invest their hearts and minds in it to the point where their morale will be affected if it's not used. The customers are well aware you're developing a prototype and will probably be able to provide more specific feedback to fine-tune the implementation. Although you may want to go back to the customer and show how responsive you were, in reality, I can expect that the customer may not be 100 percent satisfied if the delivered feature is not precisely what they want. There needs to be several rounds of going back and forth to design precisely the piece of code that fulfills the customer's requirements.

The cynics among us will provide a counter example – that prototypes will sometimes get shipped.

Some engineers often know that when they create a prototype, marketing often will look at it and say, "Ship it!" It certainly *looks* good, and it seems to satisfy the customer's basic needs, and if we bless the feature as a final release, we can announce it, declare victory, and move on to other things. Marketing may ask, "All we need to do is a minor bit of code polishing, right?"

That's not a good thing for obvious reasons. It's best to let engineers understand that a piece of prototype is expected to be thrown away, and invariably stick to that promise. If they see their prototype code being shipped to customers, they will feel a sense of shame in seeing their "half-baked" pastries fed to customers. Again, this is an issue of pride with engineers, where they do not want to see what is not their best work (or even a half serious effort) introduced to the marketplace.

What may be the result in the long-term if you release incomplete projects? Further requests for prototypes may meet resistance from engineering. Prototypes may become even less polished if your engineers see that anything that's halfway good may get shipped.

There's another way to view how engineering may react to field requests, and it's a matter of efficiency.

Inefficiency goes against an engineer's credo. So when product managers or sales managers request last-minute changes or fixes, engineers may resist, believing they are not making the best use of their time. If they see a supposedly final last-minute request before all features are frozen in a release, how does an engineer know there will not be another request a day later? Making changes to a system, especially at a fundamental level, is not unlike performing surgery. You need to open up the body, make the changes, and then spend a fair amount of time stitching and closing up the patient. There's a lot of overhead work involved, and engineers may prefer to collect a few requests and make the changes in one batch.

So a sales or marketing person may find their request for engineering to make a certain change is not immediately acted upon. The engineer may be thinking, "I'm not going to perform an appendectomy and close the patient, only to be told we need to remove the gall bladder a few hours later."

Are engineers pushing back, resisting against the firm's greater goal? Or are they making the best use of their time?

The problem here is that people are second-guessing each other. The engineers are skeptical: "They say it's a final request, but I'm certain it's not." The salespeople are wondering, "Why aren't changes being made? Aren't the engineers aware this may cost us a million-dollar deal and wreck this quarter's earnings?"

Here, I must take the engineer's side. Although both sides are at fault if plenty of second-guessing occurs, I usually see more errors in estimation from the sales side. Most people, especially those in sales, do not appreciate how much work an engineer puts into a software project. In reality, sometimes even the engineers are not aware of how difficult their work is.

When people put in last-minute requests, it's as though a restaurant patron says, "Cancel that custom-roasted turkey; I'd rather have spaghetti instead." The engineers probably have lots of other tasks to accomplish, so they are making a good tradeoff in their minds.

How does a product manager resolve this problem? The product manager's responsibility here is to gather enough requirements to help drive the development of a specification, to create good rapport with engineering, to understand the true difficulty of implementing features, to understand the effects of requests on the schedules, and to prioritize the features requests.

Ultimately, the product manager needs to take responsibility if the deliverables do not match the requirements. If sales or support did not provide enough input, then you ought to catch that oversight early enough. If engineering did not provide an accurate estimate or a detailed engineering specification where you can compare it against the customer requirements, then it is your responsibility to make sure that oversight reaches closure.

Collaboration With Focus: Extreme Programming

In general many engineers like to work in a collegial environment. People float ideas; others react to them; and the ideas are honed via constructive criticism. Most engineers are not too ego-driven (although some are), so they are happy to see the best idea win, even if it's not theirs.

After an idea is developed, it's time to actually write the program – to "code." Some engineers like to work collaboratively, and some enjoy sitting alone while they program. There are different reasons for making these choices, and people often change working styles, depending on what parts of a project they are working on.

Typically, design work needs to be collaborative, but coding and debugging are generally accepted as solitary work. Assuming this is a general rule, we find that some of the benefits of collaborative work in the design phase get lost during the implementation phase.

Rather than rely on shifting work styles, depending on phase, some engineering departments have recognized that good collaboration may be an effective way to work during *all phases* of a project.

You may ask how this relates to meeting customer requirements. One theory states that changing the organizational structure to enable rapid feedback is one effective way to close the gap between the requirements and the deliverable.

For an example, we'll use the technique known as "extreme programming," where several programmers and business analysts (who are effective product managers) sit together in a bullpen setting as the programmers, sharing a screen, write code together. The advocates of extreme programming, or XP as it is often called, state that it is an intense way of developing software, but one that is also efficient and highly effective in delivering projects on time and on target.

For details on XP, there are a number of excellent books on the market. I'm not necessarily advocating adopting this technique wholesale. Instead, I will illustrate how certain aspects of XP may succeed in closing the requirements/deliverable gap.

Some people rebel against the entire notion of XP and defend programming as fundamentally solitary tasks, where systems may be designed together, but final implementation is done independently. I admit there is a fair amount of truth in that.

On the other hand, I believe that overall, there are many aspects of the constant collaboration afforded by extreme programming that can assist direct sales software. The benefits come primarily from the interaction between product managers and engineers. (The rapid interactions among the engineers are a hallmark of XP, but they do not affect this form of software in any particular way.) There are two principal ways XP affects product management in direct sales software:

❑ An effective and efficient manner to create prototypes may allow for quicker tests from the field to validate customer requirements.

❑ Closer interactions between product managers and engineers may make the transfer of requirements to technical specifications clearer.

A warning about the use of XP: I believe XP is often successful in developing small, well-contained projects. But since the technique advocates eschewing many traditional methods of gathering requirements – such as the traditional pipeline of requirements, specifications, development, and QA – I believe XP is not appropriate as a method for managing a very large project with many interrelated pieces. I do believe XP may be effective for reacting to rapid customer requests from the field. Indeed, many customer requests tend to be feature changes on the fringe of the product, as opposed to those that require deep architectural reprogramming – changing a report, perhaps, or a user interface dialogue. Those changes are effectively small, self-contained projects.

There are many detractors of extreme programming. The reasons are many – and they stem primarily from some of its unorthodox requirements, such as having people from different disciplines sit together or incorporating QA tasks right back into engineering. These aspects that touch on organization changes have created a fair amount of resistance, so I do not think XP can or should be adopted wholesale by all organizations. If the changes were isolated as an isolated software development process, then XP would not have met as much resistance. But I sincerely believe it has kernels of ideas that can make better product management possible, so it's worth examining here.

Let's look first at some of the problems XP requirements may cause and then discuss ways it may still be adopted. It's an issue of collaboration – whether it's forced or done informally.

In extreme programming, all project members need to work in a common work area. But you don't necessarily have authority over where people sit. Perhaps your project is too large to fit into a common area, or you do not have a single room large enough for the XP bullpens.

Let's see what the benefits of XP may be adopted within your constraints. As a compromise you may want to figure out how people working in dispersed areas can learn to communicate well with each other. Being in close proximity forces people to talk to each other, overhear conversations, and communicate with coworkers informally. The goal is to find a way for all members – product managers, QA, engineers, and technical writers – to communicate with each other rapidly and effectively.

Consider the dilemma of technical writers who do not have easy access to all the technical information the engineers have. How you can enable this access through better communications? Should you do something conventional, like have more mandatory meetings, or create bonding sessions to improve team work? These ideas may work, but

I find them somewhat artificial, and they may not be sustainable.

If the writers do not mind, often it is quite effective to have them sit in an area with those working in different disciplines. This allows writers to be within earshot of other people. Although it's not as intimate as the bullpen approach, this may be the next best thing in a cubicle-based office. This arrangement creates more causal interactions, where people are literally bumping into each other, and overall it enables a better way for people to informally interact, especially groups that are typically separate.

One negative result of so much togetherness may be too much of a good thing. Many software engineers really want to focus on what they're doing. Too much "dropping by" and getting interrupted is a great way to lose concentration, and we all know losing focus for five minutes can ruin a good 30 minutes of work you have started.

In a similar way, engineers, as well as writers, are much like musicians who practice music in a focused way (which is why musicians often have special practice rooms) and artists who want to paint or draw for hours without interruption. They need to be very focused.

Some companies give software engineers individual offices with doors that actually close. Microsoft is famous for doing this, but it's the exception rather than the rule. In most Silicon Valley or Route 128 companies, you will observe oceans of cubicles.

But even in a cubicle environment, many engineers who really need to focus will find peace and quiet in any way possible. That can involve wearing headphones to shut out external noise. Some choose to display a sign to ask you not to bother them.

So how do you provide a way for people to be focused, yet at the same time prevent them from being so isolated that they don't get any interaction? Again, it's always an issue of balance, and let's look at a common dilemma.

Let's imagine you are a technical writer and want to ask a few questions to help clarify parts of a user's manual. You walk over to the cubicle of the engineer who is writing the related parts of the program, and you see that he has his headphones on and is looking intently at the screen. The natural reaction is to back off, since you do not want to interrupt him. A writer will empathize, since he's in the same situation at times. Several conflicting forces are at play here.

Software producers obviously want to create a product that has great documentation. To do so, technical writers need access to detailed technical information early on, but many writers aren't aggressive enough to want to bother the engineers who are busy writing code. The writers empathize; they are polite and respectful of the software engineer's needs.

The ideal solution is to hire a super writer who can extract information without leaving the impression that he or she bothered the engineer, but lacking that, what can you do?

Let's go back to what extreme programming was able to achieve through seating people in a common area.

Remember that an XP bullpen created mechanisms that enabled more casual meetings. People could read each other's tempo, and a lot was transferred via osmosis. Rather than create formal meetings where people are forced to share information, creating an informal environment allows people to share and be more collaborative.

So rather than regularly scheduled technical writer/ engineering meetings with a formal tone, try having brown-bag lunches, where engineering describes what's going on. Perhaps you can set up a weekly lunch meeting where people can at least voice their needs or concerns in an informal setting: "Hey, I'm a writer, and I think I'm not getting enough info. How can we resolve this?"

In summary, you really have to balance the needs for people to be ultrafocused, especially for software engineers and writers, with the need for people to interact. Try interweaving cubicles and offices, if you can, or create some other mechanism. Chance meetings that arise from neighboring offices create opportunities for casual interactions that are not perceived as intrusions. Having offices adjacent to each other allows a writer to see whether the developer has closed his debugging sessions and has taken a coffee break or is just browsing some Web sites for fun. That may be an appropriate time to "drop by" to ask some real questions.

Sales

Product managers are often at odds with salespeople. As with some conflicts between sales and engineering, the source of this conflict is often different time horizons. Salespeople tend to be short-term focused, and product managers tend to be long-term focused.

Both groups are aware their goals differ, but that does not necessarily smooth the way. Accusations such as, "Salespeople don't know anything about the product they are selling," or "Product managers don't care about actually selling the product," may fly back and forth. Product managers may accuse salespeople of selling anything – whether such a product really exists or can be delivered.

In reality, the overall long-term goal of the two groups is usually aligned – the fundamental goal is to make the firm a success.

The short-term goals are a little different. Product managers have long-term goals, as there is most often a vision about what the product ought to be, and each decision made along the way should support that long-term vision.

On the other hand, salespeople's goals are aligned with their quotas, as they ought to be. Since quotas are short-term (and whether or not they are met usually determines commission payments), sales goals are mostly short-term.

Let's listen in on a hypothetical conversation.

Project Manager: "I heard you made a sale to the Department of Defense."

Sales: "Yup. We're quite close to closing over five million dollars with the DoD."

PM: "That's great! I hadn't heard about getting close to finishing the sale. Did you need any additional help?"

Sales: "No, everything is done – initial RFP, response, etc."

PM: "What part of DoD?"

Sales: "Oh, it's hush-hush. By the way, here are their requirements. We didn't want to bother you, so we made verbal commitments to the RFP already, based on assumptions we know we can make."

PM: "I see (leafing over the RFP). Yes, I remember seeing this. By the way, you must know we don't have these features implemented yet. And it's not localized into Arabic yet. We ought to go over this before you submit the final response to the RFP."

Sales: "Details, details. I asked the engineers, and they said it was feasible. Can we deliver next month?"

PM: "Next month? And you spoke to the engineers directly?"

Sales: "The engineer said the code is Unicode enabled, so it's feasible to deliver a localized version easily."

PM: "No, no! It's an issue of whether the program is ready – as in feasible – to get localized, and that's completely different from whether we can deliver it in Arabic in short order!"

As you can see, there is a misalignment of interests. The product manager wants to be more process-oriented to create a product requirement and product plan (in this case some localization requirements), and make sure it's aligned with the product vision. But the sales rep wants to make the sale. Salespeople are bred to make sales, and their commission obviously goes up when they do. How do you align these disparate interests and goals?

In some companies product managers' objectives may have a compensation component based on overall sales of the division. Their performance is evaluated largely on their product management tasks, but part of it is tied to the sales made by their division. This will surely align the objectives, but often at some cost to an overall vision, and it may make parts of product management highly reactive to short-term needs to the detriment of the longer-term strategy.

Let's consider some other ways we can bridge this gap.

Product managers with some sales experience tend to understand the needs of sales. On the other hand, I've seen an unusual amount of friction arise between sales and highly technical product managers, as well as between sales and engineering groups. Engineering staff, particularly those with only a few years of industry experience, may show some distaste for what they perceive as salespeople's flashiness or smooth talking.

Although that may run counter to an engineer's ethos, an engineer should recognize that salespeople behave that way to do their jobs effectively. It's important for technical people to see beyond these surface characteristics and see how they can assist in performing a job.

By definition, salespeople have chosen to be in sales jobs because they are good at selling things and continue to be successful each year. It's a self-selecting process. Good salespeople can listen to and understand a customer's needs and know how to align those needs with a product's offering. Although a good salesperson will work hard to close a deal, in reality their job is to work through a range of prospects and narrow the field to the few who provide the highest probability of making a sale. They are highly efficient and opportunistic. Rarely does a salesperson try to "force" a product on a prospect who is not receptive. It just isn't worth their time or effort.

Salespeople go through different phases throughout the year. Quarter-end and year-end tend to be especially stressful as they try to fill their quotas. Engineers should be able to understand this stress, since they go through similar cycles in product releases. So at certain times of the year you will hear more from salespeople, but with different agendas. Basically, the agenda swings from long-term needs to short-term needs.

When a sales deal will put the rep's quota over the top, they may ask for special favors, such as adding a few special features, to make the sale. They are aware that engineers cannot actually deliver substantial changes in a matter of weeks. Sometimes they are looking for commitments to make larger changes; at other times, small cosmetic changes enable a deal to close.

But the downside is that making a large collection of requests may slow down product development and release, and the ultimate tradeoff may be to increase one sales group's commission at the risk of decreasing it for many more. The net effect may be negative. The mistake made by some product managers is trying to make all the tradeoff decisions alone, rather than conferring with sales managers on prioritizing requests. The sales managers have the big picture; they know the probability of each deal closing, and whether it's worth putting the effort into it. Although you cannot rely on the sales manager completely for making the decision, since the product manager does own the product, the sales manager's input is too important to neglect.

This mistake is less likely to happen if a sales manager proactively prioritizes the requests and feeds the list to product management. Problems occur when individual sales reps contact product managers to further their agenda.

At other times of the year, when sales reps and systems engineers are not under tremendous quota pressure, they present an unusually rich insight into product needs from a true customer perspective. Those are the times when collaboration can occur without a large amount of friction. Short-term or personal orientation may cloud the picture of the "greater good." It's all a matter of different perspectives of sales and product management. It's unfortunate when the parties come to loggerheads just because they focus on their differences and neglect their shared goals.

To make things work better between the two groups, product managers need to realize that sales is an excellent channel for understanding customer needs. The worst thing would be for the product manager to step back, become detached from the marketplace, and believe he knows best what the customer wants. That's a step toward failure. Although a product manager may visit a customer once in a while, or he may have taken a few surveys or led a few focus groups, the field or salespeople are in front of customers day to day, getting their ears full of complaints, requests, and advice.

Even when the customer does not understand the true benefits of the product, sales can still gain valuable input from them. The sales rep can test ideas against them and try to understand why certain new features are not fully used or appreciated. This information can be delivered to engineering and considered for future changes to the product. Sales reps shouldn't consider product managers a roadblock to sales, or a bureaucratic layer; sales reps should consider product managers as partners.

It's in the sales reps' interest to get things done for their customers to close the pending deal, but they need to realize each request may result in a delay of a product release, and that each late product may result in a deal that cannot close on time.

Ideally there is a great amount of collaboration, and most important is setting the right expectations.

If there's a large and important deal in the works, but the sales or supports needs are complex, sales should alert the product managers and engineers so there will be adequate preparation.

Let the product managers (and other relevant areas of the company) consider the tradeoffs of making a special accommodation to one particular customer:

❑ Will the product modification to make one customer happy be worthwhile (financially)?

❑ Will they be a good long-term customer? Will they be a great reference to leverage additional deals?

❑ Will the deal result in good PR, based on the respect this customer commands in the trade press? Will they provide a testimonial?

❑ Will the deal enhance your competitive position?

Support

Support staff, such as customer support or telephone support, give great insight into reality. This group is often neglected, but plays a critical role in supporting sales and providing under-the-radar testing of the product – either on their own or by conveying field test results to engineering groups. Incidentally, the pre-sales or sales engineers are placed in a separate category, although they are sometimes (accidentally) categorized as part of the support staff.

Product managers may often view support requests as complaints, but little do they know that support is a true window into reality, as opposed to the rose-colored view that marketing people like to portray. It's unfortunate that some people have the perception that support is a source of complaints, but there is a grain of truth to the perception. Very few customers call support with a word of thanks and a pat on the back. Instead, they call to complain about the product. So the helpdesk or support database naturally accumulates plenty of complaints.

Since people don't like to listen to complaints, it's easy to place yourself in a frame of mind to filter them out. But doing so is a form of denial that blinds you to the reality occurring in the customers' offices.

Who would you rather listen to?

❑ Salespeople, who may not even talk to the real users, since they are concentrating on "business issues"?

❑ PR or marketing people, who give you filtered views from analysts (which are important for other reasons but certainly don't reflect what a user really wants)?

❑ Analysts, who may have some great corporate insight and top-level, strategic viewpoints on what the product ought to do for the company 10 years from now?

What about trying to resolve a customer complaint right now?

Support staff can provide you with a wealth of information. Great support people will maintain a support database, deduce information from it, and provide excellent reports.

It may be possible to deduce trends, get statistics on which support incidents are frequently encountered, and have a set of real-world data to base future product planning on. Naturally, positive experiences may not be recorded in a support incident database, but the data of the negative experiences in the database will give you insight and numeric data to back up product improvement decisions.

Marketing

Marketing folks wear multiple hats, depending on the company and often even within a company, so it's hard to categorize them into one group. Naturally, people with different tasks have different motivations.

Marketing people are driven by motivations as diverse as:

❑ Advertisement or brand awareness needs
❑ Press releases to create buzz or mentions
❑ Industry analysts' opinions
❑ Presence at events and trade shows

Needs vary, and time horizons vary greatly. Some things, such as analyst tours and product reviews, may be deadline-driven, and work for major trade show events usually moves at a frantic pace. Although events are planned months in advance, they have their share of deadlines just before and during the show.

It's hard to create a single profile of these stakeholders and their behavior and motivations. Yet it's interesting to note that these stakeholders often need to collaborate, and given the variance in their motivations, may easily create friction. My only advice here is to allocate enough slack time or resources for short-term marketing needs and look at your calendar to remind yourself the long-term requirements.

Let's look at a product announcement as a central rallying point as we discuss marketing.

The emphasis in a product announcement "push" can be determined by the motivations of the team leaders, the corporate culture, or a combination of both. Some companies are marketing-driven; their "splash" has high priority. Other companies are engineering-driven; they may produce relatively quiet announcements with a relentless push to get the product into the hands of influential technical users. In general a company that places more emphasis on a splashy announcement will give more power to the outbound marketing staff.

Naturally, the people on the marketing side have needs and motivations that are different from the product manager side. In some companies the people who do outbound marketing differ from the product managers involved in inbound marketing by belonging in physically different groups.

An outbound marketing group in a large company may constantly be marketing products from different groups as they arrive in waves that chase each other. I call this the specialist marketing group. In others, one group is expected to shift gears to spend time in marketing activities. These people escort a product from inception to release. I call this the jack-of-all-trades group. Which is better? Nobody falls 100 percent into one camp or the other. Frequently, a specialist may assist a jack-of-all-trades as they work to launch a product.

A problem arises, in my opinion, in a mismatch, where a product with a certain characteristic is matched with a launch group with the wrong focus. For example, a marketing communications–oriented launch group may spend a lot of time on data sheets, but not enough on analysts.

If a communications and PR group is brought in for focused assistance during a launch, then things may work out. But if such a group is given the responsibility for the entire product management task, then there will be a great mismatch and loss of focus. For example, you can get an ill-defined product because much of the group's energies are focused on collateral, but the product requirements for engineering get little attention.

Let's consider the pros and cons of each type of person who is involved:

A marketing person who is a jack-of-all-trades and is therefore a general product manager tends to bring more passion to a product, since they feel a long-term ownership of the product. They can bring in-depth knowledge and a history of a product's development to its launch.

The specialists provide much knowledge of the trade press, the idiosyncrasies of the analysts, and other items of which a jack-of-all-trades does not have deep knowledge. They may have a good understanding of the requirements of creating a brand and communicating it to the audience.

But being an overly outbound person may cause some problems. Some people want to do frequent press releases to create buzz. That attitude reached its peak during the late 1990s' technology bubble, when all people wanted was publicity and ink, no matter whether there was enough substance to back it up.

Emphasis on Buzz, Analysis, and Events

We've all heard stories about writers for technical magazines or newspapers who receive countless press releases and announcements in their e-mail boxes every day – perhaps as much as several hundred. The result is that no one has time to read it all. They realize much of it is fluff, perhaps unrelated to what they write about, so they delete it sight unseen. The press release–driven culture backfired and devalued the importance of truly newsworthy events.

Other people are analyst-driven. Analysts do not deal with short-term news, but tend to focus on long-term trends and analysis. Marketing people who have a strong emphasis on analysts are extremely eager to get as much interaction as possible with software industry analysts from firms such as Meta Group or Gartner Group.

These marketing people require more substance to have a meaningful discussion and careful knowledge of each analyst's view of the industry and the competitive landscape, so they can position your product or firm in the context of the industry that the analysts view. Given an analyst's preoccupation with competitive positioning and the value a software product provides a customer, caring enough to gain the attention of analysts tends to align the marketing needs with the product development needs. But it's easy to go overboard, being drawn into the 20,000-foot level analysis of the product and market segment, and losing sight of pragmatic, short-term needs, such as assisting sales.

Some outbound marketing staff favor big events or big launches. This may mean participation in trade shows or specialized events driven by the firm. It's rare, however, to find a marketing person who is totally driven by the need to market a product through events.

In any case, the importance of tradeshows seems to have waned in the past few years. Over the years the glut of tradeshows has made each of them less important. And easy access to information and downloadable demonstration systems through the Net has made going to a live conference hall increasingly less important. But some types of software that are retail store–oriented do have a strong tie to major industry trade shows, as we will discuss later.

How do these types of outbound marketing fare in light of increased commoditization of software? I see some conflicting signals from the industry. If you examine the marketing activities of low-priced, commodity software that is beginning to encroach on the previously proprietary software segments, you'll notice they do not seem to spend money on marketing.

The attitude seems to be, "Here's a product that does just as much as competitor X, and it costs Y percent less." However, I also suspect that competing on price alone is a suicidal approach, since price becomes the sole differentiator. I suspect that, eventually, marketing and brand-awareness will start to play an ever increasing role. During the late 1990s' boom, excessive funds were spent on marketing to capture the consumer's mind-share. Consumer goods have traditionally relied on brand marketing campaigns to position themselves. Will commodity software marketing become just like dog food marketing? I doubt it, since there is still plenty of room for innovation. The products are inherently more complex, with more facets where products can differentiate in a fundamental way.

Different types of software require different types of marketing. The right blend depends on the product, the market segment, and the general strategy for the product. Let's examine the spectrum of emphasis for product management, ranging from being very product-oriented to being outbound marketing–oriented.

Much retail software has a natural tendency toward heavy outbound marketing. For example, games are most often released with big product launches. The reason is that the motivations for purchases by retail stores and ultimately the end-consumers are quite different from those of a conventional enterprise.

It's true that in the long term, the product content is most important. In games, ultimately, the "playability" and enjoyment are paramount.

Yet in many ways these products resemble modern movies more than technical enterprise software. Word of mouth, impulse purchase, and an aura of enjoyment contribute significantly to initial sales. So a splashy launch associating the product with celebrity endorsements, combined with a good reputation built by earlier product versions from the publishers, will often encourage strong seasonal orders.

If you're creating games, it may be that the E^3, the Electronic Entertainment Expo, is an almost mandatory venue to exhibit a game product. And what happens at these shows? You see lots of glitz and hoopla – not too different from events that hype a movie opening.

Collaboration of Inbound and Outbound Marketing

Frequently there's friction between outbound and inbound product management. As usual, this stems from different motivations. The inbound person tends to think long-term, while the outbound person is looking for publicity.

Sometimes the issue boils down to having people's calendars coordinated. If you are not completely synchronizing the outbound marketing calendars with the inbound product manager's schedule, you can get into this type of trouble.

Somebody in outbound marketing says, "Hey, big issues of *Info World* and *Computerworld* are focusing on topic XYZ – can we create a demo in time? Can we move up the release date?" The inbound product manager wants to accommodate these requests, but some deadlines are just impossible to meet.

If your development group works diligently to meet a certain deadline, and a seemingly random – but significantly high-impact – request gets thrown onto the production calendar, the entire schedule can get thrown into chaos.

Constant and close collaboration with outbound marketing requests, especially those that affect the production calendar, should be mandatory. This means you have to be very methodical about requirements, both long-term and short-term, with enough time set aside for developing demos, to allow everyone to plan ahead. Even software demos need to be carefully designed, constructed, tested, and distributed, so outbound marketing can't expect them to materialize overnight.

Events and PR: Important or Not?

If PR and special promotional events are highly relevant for your product, it is crucial that their significance is known and understood by your entire team.

If you publish games, and an Entertainment Expo is looming on your calendar, realize that show on the calendar is your team's primary driver. Make sure the date is fixed on your production calendar and that everybody on the team respects its significance and ensures their priorities are all based on the appropriate ship date. Most mature employees are aware of these priorities, but it's possible for some people to ignore the facts and get their priorities confused.

Direct sales software places comparatively less emphasis on outbound marketing. Analysts are relatively more important, given their influence on corporate decision-makers.

Decide who will go on your analyst tour. You can't afford to make this a "fluffy" presentation. It has to be very direct regarding your product's features and benefits to ensure you get the right kind of analysis for your product.

Finance

Financial considerations can never be ignored, even in direct sales software.

My technical background may create a bias here, but I believe financial models can both help and create problems for your product. I am referring to having financial support for resource allocation for the product, whether for development or product support.

Let's eavesdrop on another hypothetical conversation.

Finance: "We need to lower the costs in these cost centers."

Product Manager: "Oh? Like in what areas?"

Fin: "We are spending a whole lot in support."

PM: "Yes, we had a complex product launch."

Fin: "Can we cut support hours? Can we charge more for support?"

PM: "People need support!"

Fin: "Oh, the doc kits. They are a large component of the COGS (cost of goods sold). Can we eliminate the doc kits and make it all online?"

PM: "Argh!"

The lesson, of course, is a difference in the time horizon each person is concerned with. Finance is looking closely at costs, while product management is concerned with long-term satisfaction. The example may sound like a joke, but realistically we've all seen products that have eliminated doc kits, and now we can't figure out how to use the software.

It is crucial to work with the finance groups to reach a common understanding of what costs are required to advance sales, and not treat these costs as components that drive margins up or down.

What was finance's motivation? On the surface, it's obvious they wanted to lower the cost of goods sold (COGS). A person who may be classically trained to increase margins will look at any way to lower the COGS.

Yet, since software has such high incremental margins, it's important to look at the big picture. It's regrettable that people try to trim costs where incremental savings really do not contribute greatly to the overall margins.

Continuing with the example of the documentation kits, we see that large, established software companies often make available a set of books separately, perhaps from their technical press division or in collaboration with an outside publisher. In reality, I suspect that many customers do not purchase those extra books immediately. They may have a frustrating experience early, and be driven to buy the book later on, but the lasting impression of a bad initial experience may linger.

On the positive side, there are cases where finance can give you great insight into the overall profit-and-loss model for the product. For example, it is worthwhile to consider the variable costs. We know that in software the R&D costs are more or less constrained as fixed costs.

But support and post-release engineering costs may sometimes vary by the number of units you sell. Support costs will obviously increase according to the number of support calls. And even bug-fix, post-release engineering is a function of the number of bugs reported.

Finance questions that will assist in proper product development may include:

❏ What can be done in the product to control support costs and also keep the customers satisfied?

❏ What can you do to fix the problems early on so that people do not need to call support?

STAKEHOLDERS

IN PACKAGED SOFTWARE

The stakeholders in packaged software are mostly the same as in direct sales software, and many of the issues are similar to those in direct sales software. This chapter will emphasize the major differences.

Engineering

Engineering needs for packaged software are still great. The talents of engineers and software engineers are always at a premium, and they are always stretched thin.

Engineers' ability to create product is the source of any product management task. Since packaged software tends to be released in a more predictable manner than direct sales software, the product development tasks can be performed in a more a disciplined manner, because a fixed product-release schedule allows for better planning.

Normally, engineers are not pulled in at the last moment to make changes and fixes for one customer. We do need to realize, however, that even in packaged software, there are large customers who hold great influence and may request the creation of special editions.

Although the "real-time" demands for support and patches after a product release aren't imposed for packaged-software engineers, other demands are just as challenging. The demand to create a solid product on a fixed release schedule may not be a great blessing. If you are creating a piece of enterprise software, there are inevitable schedule delays. You cannot always predict when a product will ship. To some extent, you ship when the product is ready. In the case of a packaged product, which obviously includes the games category, you need to rely on announcement or shipment dates (such as a large entertainment software show or a holiday gift-buying schedule). If you somehow underestimated the effort required to finish a piece of code, the deadline becomes very scary, and people may have to work many long overtime hours to meet it.

Tech Publications

Skimping on hiring or other resources for documentation and tech publications is like skimping on security for a heavy-metal concert.

Software isn't like a car. Nobody can just step in and drive it away. Your customers need to be guided, taught by books, online, help files – whatever works best with the software you create. So the investment in documentation can create a big payoff in lower support costs, easier sales, and higher customer satisfaction.

It is extremely important for packaged software to have good documentation. Unlike direct sales, no one will be on hand to give your customers a personal demo, an individualized training session, or abundant telephone support time. They are alone, or reliant on just-as-clueless friends for help, and support calls may cost you money. Ensure that adequate resources are provided for writers and that they are always given access to any information they need.

Writers tend to work well in packaged software with fixed dates. And the good ones give accurate estimates on how long it will take and how difficult it will be to meet your requirements, so don't try to outguess them. Also, do not try to do the writing yourself or have anyone else who is not a professional writer create the documentation. It's harder than it looks.

Sales

There's always a role for direct sales, even in packaged software. In many packaged-software firms, there's still a direct sales team that makes big deals. For example, large enterprises may purchase copies of products such as Adobe® Acrobat® in large volumes.

There are constraints that make it difficult for sales, the primary one being that there is little control over features once the product has shipped. There is less of a chance to do a special patch release. It is sometimes possible to create a special edition for customers after the initial or first revenue ship of a product, but this is often reserved for the most important customers.

Sales teams, even in packaged software, will certainly try to get the product manager's attention to voice their requests for features or fixes they feel are necessary to close certain deals. This poses a difficult issue for packaged-product managers. Should you listen to them carefully, or they do reflect a narrow sliver of the total field of customers?

Let's look at the pros and cons of dealing with "real" customers in getting requirements for a packaged software product. A product manager can gain input for requirements for a retail product in several ways. Here are some compromises that may work for packaged software.

A product manager can perform widespread market research or surveys. But I often find the surveys tend to display a cold, impersonal view of the potential customer base. It's difficult to rally people around abstract statistics. In the same way it's hard to visualize an average family with 2.2 children; the product staff of support, writers, engineers, and outbound marketing people cannot easily develop or market a product for an abstract "spends two hours a day on PC" customer.

So an easy, even lazy, potential way to solve this problem is to talk to the direct sales team and get hooked up to live customers. You must keep in mind, however, that the direct sales team represents only a certain fraction of your sales. If you pay a disproportionate share of your attention to them, you may neglect the true market segment you are targeting.

It's easy to talk to a direct sales customer (or sales or systems engineers, who act as intermediaries). All you need to do is call. But how do you deal with the other 90 percent, or perhaps the other 99 percent, of your customers? You do want to oil the squeaky wheel, but how do you find a balance?

That skill comes from experience. The ideal case is to find a real, live customer who often matches the ideal characteristics. There's a saying in politics: "As New Hampshire goes, so goes the nation."

Is it possible to find such a customer? My favorite solution is to rely on quantifiable survey results to get reliable data, but then you create a persona that represents the data. Such a persona is easy to rally around. You can put a face on the potential customer by creating a fictitious person, complete with a name and a profile – Novice Nancy, Junior Johnny, Expert Ellen, and so on, with associated skills, knowledge, and usage characteristics. Are they stereotyped? Yes, they are often over-the-top characterizations of people they represent, but putting a face on these profiles allows engineers, sales reps, and others to visualize their customers.

Channels

Products sold through indirect sales channels actually provide interesting problems regarding how you can create a product that motivates the sales channel. It's not simply an issue of sales promotions, training, incentives, and other classic items that define channel management. Issues involve answering (among others) such questions as:

❏ Can the channel support it adequately?
❏ How can the right resources be found to support it?
❏ Can they add the right value to increase their margins?

In general you can simplify the issues faced by the indirect channels by answering one question: Will it make the cash register ring?

The channel, such as VARs, is small businesses, and they have many choices of products to sell and support. Finding a way to increase their bottom line is the right way to motivate the reseller channels. If you add features, such as increased supportability, to a product, then you ought to position it in a way to appeal to their net income.

The Voice of Your Customer?

In addition to surveys there are lots of ways to find the voices of other customers. Working with the support staff is a good way to get direct input, and you can also take random lists from product registration and approach them directly. The support staff can often identify certain customers who are good at finding bugs or voicing needs or concerns ahead of other customers. These "canaries in the coal mine" are precious and should be treated with respect and care.

If the retail or some other indirect channel, such as a VAR channel, plays a role in your distribution, you can contact them, as well.

Retail

Dealing with retailers is difficult, since they are several steps removed from the producers of software. They sell so many other products that it's difficult to have them provide adequate feedback. But perhaps you can use them as a convenient venue to gather user feedback.

You can play "secret shopper" by pretending to be a customer in a retail shop, talking to the salespeople to see how they sell and explain your product. By knowing what they know and don't know, you can understand how the competition fares and how your positioning statement works. At the end you can reveal your identify to initiate a discussion of specific sales tools they need.

Discussions With User Groups

User groups are great places to meet true fans or enthusiasts for your product. Nowhere else will you meet people who have as much knowledge of or passion for your product. But you must be prepared before you start visiting their meetings. Have you seen the movie *Gladiator?* Do you know what it means to be thrown to the lions? These are highly knowledgeable folks, and you can't dance around on stage when you aren't ready for them.

Marketing

Marketing obviously plays a more important role in packaged software. The bulk of your product's awareness building, brand building, and therefore demand generation is built up through marketing programs. I won't discuss this in detail, as conventional marketing differs from the primary focus of this book.

Support

Customer support plays a large role in retail software. With the lack of direct customer contact via sales, customer support staff are often the eyes and ears of the customers.

Without a direct sales force as customer advocates, it's easy to become complacent and start to think you know what's best for your customer. Formalized market research and focus groups and surveys are all good, but they sometimes give you only fluffy, soft views on needs.

Take focus groups for example. The participants you get to meet are people who have the free time to collect the $100 incentive given to attend the focus group as potential customers. Or they are temps gathered at the last moment to do usability testing. Do they accurately reflect your true customers? I think not, and it's dangerous to put too much weight on them.

On the other hand, people who call support are real users who care enough to vent their problems. If you've ever needed to listen to people who are willing to be articulate and vocal, here's your chance to find them.

WHAT MAKES A GOOD
PRODUCT MANAGER?

What makes a good product manager? A snap answer is to say it's being a manager. Attributes that make anybody a good manager apply to good software product management, as well.

Product managers interact with a wide variety of people in sales, manufacturing, marketing communications, technical writing, and engineering. But unlike a traditional manager, you typically do not have authority over them.

Product management groups often have their own hierarchy, but nevertheless, the vast majority of the people you have to deal with are people you don't have authority over. You can't necessarily delegate responsibilities to them; you just have to influence them to do things.

By ensuring people understand common goals, you can ensure the right things get done, and they all work as a team. In that context, let's discuss a variety of things that make a good manager.

Trust

The role of a product manager is often visualized as the hub of a wheel, with spokes reaching out to other parties. You need to trust other people to do the right things because by definition, you don't know as much about the work as the people who are doing the work.

If you had worked your way up to manager in a bakery or foreman in the factory, you would probably have done the actual work before. So the people who now report to you in the bakery or the factory look to you, their manager, for guidance on dealing with details about their jobs. If you're a master baker who manages a bakery, an apprentice baker would ask you, "How do I do this? Am I kneading my dough right?" If you're a foreman in the factory, and one of your employees doesn't know how to deal with a problem with something going on down the assembly line, they could ask you for help.

Some product managers may have had experience as engineers or in sales; you could have some experience in understanding the technical issues. But as technology evolves, you start to lose detailed knowledge. You really cannot know the technology as well as the engineers.

You obviously have to place trust in the engineer to do that job right. This comes from hiring the right people originally – and that may not be within your control. You have placed trust in the engineering managers in hiring their own teams. Sometimes you have influence in the hiring process, but that's not always true.

Let's imagine what happens when you start losing trust.

As someone who admits to not having the experience and technology knowledge, let's say you start to nose in on and question decisions that an engineer has made. You realize it's not an area of your expertise, but you start to second-guess people. Then you immediately start to create animosity or mistrust.

This is somewhat similar to micromanaging. You really have to trust your team: "You do what you do best, and I'll do what I do best." That builds teamwork and helps create the ability to work with people with whom you interact without authority.

Loyalty

By trusting people to know what they're doing, you also build loyalty among them. You also have to be loyal, since you are at the center of this wheel with the spokes coming out, and you need to be loyal to people you may not have direct authority over. Since you rely on them, you need to realize they rely on you, and you need to stand up for their needs. If people you deal with follow their own good judgment, and you trust them, then you need to stand up for them.

What do you do if a writer comes to you and says he doesn't have enough information to create the documentation for the product in time, or if an engineer tells you she's being asked to deliver something that isn't quite ready yet?

Let's say this results in a delay in the product schedule, over which you have influence, and you realize this delay will cause friction with sales. You decide to stand up for these people, since you trust their abilities and their assessments, and, therefore, that they made the right choice. Your decision to support them will generate loyalty in the future because you demonstrated trust and respect for them.

Fair Decision-making

You need to separate clearly the company goals, personal goals, and politics. Sales may have great motivation to fulfill a quota. It's an effective incentive, but sometimes their personal goals may conflict with some of the company goals. You don't want to make a decision that favors one sales representative, which may in turn harm the sales of other reps.

You or the sales manager needs to stand back and determine whether you are pushing the company goal forward or effectively pushing forward the requirements of one person.

The latter may be viewed as a political thing, since it allowed personal needs to rise to the surface. It may be simply a problem of ensuring proper features are placed into the product, which is part of a well-defined product management and requirements management process. But outsiders may view it as a process that's politicized and influenced by personal relationships. Then people start to distrust the process you put in place to define a product and release it.

Perhaps you have in place a process for gathering product requirements documents, marketing requirements documentation, a release plan, and so on. If people trust an impartial and effective process, it becomes a well-run machine.

But the moment people perceive a politicized process where things are being juggled around for personal reasons, then the process itself is in question. People stop trusting the precise release dates and milestones you have positioned. It's immensely important to make sure decision-making is fair and is *perceived* as fair.

Collaboration

Since a product manager doesn't have authority over all the people creating a product, a large amount of collaboration is required. Software, just like any other product, is a collaborative endeavor, and you are in the middle, trying to coordinate this collaborative teamwork. Software tends to be more difficult in the sense that it is more of an artistic endeavor, where things are a lot less well-defined, compared to old-fashioned manufacturing.

Although you are at the hub of the wheel, you cannot afford to insist all information and decision-making go through you. You need to create a process where all the "spokes can talk to each other." Yet, you don't want everyone to have to talk to everyone else. You don't want the engineering people to be constantly talking to the salespeople, and the salespeople talking to the technical publications staff.

What's the right balance? You can't become the bottleneck, where everyone's view of the development process is made through the small window of the product manager. But neither do you want chaos, where there are thousands of different channels of communications and multiple channels of decision-making.

People need to be focused and know you can perform the right amount of collaboration, and not be distracted by secondary decisions being made.

At the same time, however, it's good to create a collaborative atmosphere, where everyone knows what everyone else is doing. It's sometimes good to create a collaborative atmosphere by sponsoring "show and tell" events.

These various events will enable the writers who are writing technical publications to hear a presentation from customer support and hear how the books are used. They get a better understanding of who reads the books, and improvements may be made. And engineers can get feedback on how users actually use their programs. Such a collaborative atmosphere creates a strong esprit de corps within the software development and marketing organizations as well, and enforces an understanding of the high-level goals.

Motivation

Motivation is the incentives that drive people. The motivation of sales reps is clearly the desire to fulfill their quotas. With engineers and technical writers, and even with marketing, the answer is less clear. Sometimes, the motivators come from the least expected places. I'll show you a few examples; then you can work out the motivators of the members of your own team.

Motivation goes back to the issue of work style, and the answers are not black-and-white.

Technical writers are often motivated by the opportunity to write and rewrite a good piece of work. At other times, seeing clear evidence of how their work is being appreciated is a great motivator. Getting concrete feedback is important. Creating a good feedback loop is very important to them as well.

For engineers, who tend to work in an abstract world of source code and software design, the basic motivation is making a good design and writing code that's correct, fast, compact, and feature-rich.

But sometimes, seeing something tangible that turns their source code into a real product may bring joy to engineers. If you are a product manager in retail software, here are a couple of small things that bring engineers an unexpected feeling of accomplishment:

❑ Data sheet that calls out their favorite technology or feature

❑ Product package prototypes with user manual, CD-ROM, and other items

It's often great to ask a variety of people for some feedback. Does this box look right? Does this datasheet communicate the right message? You don't necessarily want every single group to have input, but when engineers provide feedback into product packaging, it increases their sense of ownership, and you can catch mistakes, since they know the product in detail, and they may be able to point out incorrect descriptions.

When people see their C++ program finally turn into something tangible, it's a way to see the fruits of their labor become real. As much as software engineers work in an abstract world of code, they're still people who really get excited by seeing something physical.

As a thank-you gift, it's good to give each member the physical product itself. They can place it on their bookshelf as a trophy. It sounds trivial, but it costs very little, and it's a worthwhile keepsake. In other industries, people have similar keepsakes. Financiers often get trophies for the deals they've made. Writers can point to book covers, and recording artists display their records and CDs.

Common Goals

Let's discuss management by goals as opposed to micromanagement. People make the right decisions when given the right goals.

Technical writers know they're not writing a book to sell, but instead they understand clearly their goal to write a manual to complement the product.

Engineers are one step removed, where their immediate work does not necessarily translate easily from their group's goals.

Let's use the example of the management report we used earlier. If the requirements for the management report are not adequately shown, the engineering group may make their own set of assumptions. If sufficient basic requirements are shown to engineers or designers, then they can build on that foundation and make all their decisions from it. If the purpose of the management report is to present a high-level summary, then the engineers can make all decisions – font, colors, interaction components, and layout – to further that goal. So there is no need to ask for validation on each design point.

In ancient times, before rapid communications became possible, Rome managed to rule a far-flung empire. You certainly couldn't have people in Rome constantly communicating with their outposts in Northern Europe. The round-trip communications would have taken too long for effective management. Instead, the local rulers knew the goals and missions.

Once the manager knows that all the team members know the goals, and that the each sub-goal is aligned with the corporate goal, you can rest assured that people will make the right decisions, and then people don't have to come to you for verification and understanding each time.

As a product manager in the middle of all these different elements, you want to make sure the goals you communicate to the employees are aligned with the high-level goals of your company. So you are a representative of the business unit manager, product unit manager, or your divisional manager, or even the CEO's goals.

If the goals are polluted by hidden personal goals, then you can spread confusion, since the alignment between goals is not transparent, and there is some perception of mismatch between a sub-goal and a corporate goal.

By establishing common goals for the product, you don't have to micromanage people. Common goals for a product may be very general, such as "Ease of use" or "Highest performance and reliability."

If you emphasize ease of use as a theme, then obviously the writers will emphasize the ease of use in the manuals. The engineers will put a lot of effort into making the user interface easy to use, and that feedback is placed into different parts of the interaction model.

These are common management hints that any manager has to worry about. But this is especially important for software product management because you don't have direct authority, and the goals in a software product are often ambiguous.

Deliverables of

a Product Manager

The following items are not all required for all product managers, and they may have different names in various companies. As we review them, consider them from the perspective of your company's culture and processes.

Market Requirements Document (MRD)

You want a market requirements document that answers the following questions: What do the customers want? What are their problems? Some people call this a vision document. It should be the first document, written before any specification is written.

You're not necessarily suggesting a solution or an implementation here. You are stating the requirements. What's required? What's optional? What's nice to have? Who is the audience?

You can perform some market research, but don't go overboard, since you can't talk to everyone, and it's very expensive. On the other hand, you don't want to base your requirements on just a few people you randomly choose.

It's great to get a set of trusted advisors to form an advisory council. These people should be visionaries, with lots of experience, and after many interactions with them, you'll see some patterns you may choose to pursue.

If you are creating a complex piece of software that's sold to a large and widely divergent group of customers, then you will probably use some formal market research based on a large sample size.

Building this document is no different from creating some new form of dog food. You can't base your decisions solely on your cocker spaniel and the toy poodle next door, and you need to know what the dog population is willing to chow down.

Parts of a requirements document include:

1. *Background:* What's this project all about? We need to present the business case.

2. *Product Position:* Positioning statement that tells how the product distinguishes itself in the marketplace. A product manager can do this, or work with marketing on it.

3. *Target Customer:* Categorize the type of customer by market segment or customer profile.

4. *Competition:* Name companies that may sell into your space, including not only existing ones, but also those that can move in.

5. *Potential Customers:* Who may actually buy this (especially if you are targeting the enterprise Fortune 500 market)?

6. *Functional Requirements:* List how the product is supposed to function and behave.

7. *Schedule Requirements:* When must you ship it? This is not strictly part of the requirements process, but a general idea of a schedule is required.

Product Requirements Document (PRD)

This is sometimes joined with the MRD, specifying the product in detail. It should discuss the direct experience the end-user will have.

You can accomplish this via mockups, sample output, behavioral descriptions, etc. You do not need to specify what goes underneath the covers, since that is an implementation issue best addressed by engineering.

Here are some suggestions for what you can do to describe product requirements:

❏ If the product has an extensive user interface, you can provide a mockup that you and a designer can create with graphic design tools.

❏ Use simple graphics created with tools like Microsoft Visio or Adobe Photoshop. If you have less time, it can be as simple as a hand-drawn diagram.

❑ As simple as a hand-drawn diagram may be, it's certainly better than ambiguous verbal descriptions, or vaguely worded specifications.

❑ If you have more time, you can try to create an interactive prototype using Visual Basic or some other tool.

❑ If the product does not have an extensive user interface, you need to describe it in functional terms. This is usually a technical document that may describe program behavior, with specific performance characteristics, etc.

Functional Requirements Document (FRD)

Engineering writes the functional requirements based on the PRD and the MRD.

The FRD addresses the precise deliverable from engineering, including the exact deliverable, the schedules the product manager and engineering need to agree on, functional specifics, etc. There needs to be a seamless understanding between the product manager and the engineering group on what is to be delivered.

Remember that it may be impossible to state the requirements at an extremely fine level because you need to be responsive to market needs, but the overall goals and direction need to be set.

Schedules

Working together with engineering, support, and the technical writers, the product manager drives the creation of the schedule that includes the following:

1. Engineering development
2. Documentation (offline and online) delivery
3. Beta tests
4. Support
   ❑ Training for support and sales engineering
   ❑ Should include any support for Beta tests
5. Post-release patch release, if appropriate

6. Planning for end-of-life of previous product versions, if
    any

7. Managing the release process

This is the day-to-day management of dealing with each
issue as the product gets developed. The tasks are so varied
that it is difficult to name all the things you could
anticipate, but let's discuss some highlights.

The Release Process

One of the key tasks of the release process is to squash
software bugs. You can claim this is an engineering task,
but product management ultimately needs to work closely
with engineering on this, and in some cases, drives the
meetings to discuss the bugs.

In this process you need to create a prioritized list of all
known problems, according the severity standards you and
engineering have agreed on. It may include items such as:

Severity	What Happens
Showstopper	Can't release product without fixing this
Severity 1	Prevents product from working
Severity 2	Prevents product from working some of the time
Future Enhancement	Not required in the initial release

Eventually you are like a field doctor trying to perform triage. You simply do not have the resources to address all problems, and fixing some lesser known bugs may need to be deferred until a patch release, or the next version.

Beta Management

Beta management is a complex task that addresses both engineering and sales needs. This includes areas such as:

❏ *Working with sales to recruit good beta sites:* The needs often conflict, since you want to get good customers who can exercise the product to discover bugs, but sales may not want such customers to participate if they do not have the testing resources. It's a careful balance, where the beta customer must be willing and able to assist you, and you need to return some favors to them by ensuring the specific needs or requirements they uncover during the beta are fixed in the final release.

❏ *Getting legal documents in order,* so the beta software doesn't leak out or create a liability if it crashes.

❏ *Releasing the beta:* You are in effect doing a mini-release, so you need to consider production issues, which may be an online download or production of a CD-ROM.

❏ *Making documentation available:* The difficulty, of course, is that the documentation is still in production, so it is incomplete. You need to recognize that support from SEs may be required to install the product accurately.

❏ *Preparing the support staff:* The beta product may require telephone support to use it, and there needs to be a mechanism for gathering bug reports that, in turn, get fed back into engineering.

❏ *Taking feedback* from the beta customers through multiple sources (support, online), prioritizing it, and then incorporating it back into the development process.

In many ways this is a good trial run to the actual product release, since it gets many things debugged out of the system. You are debugging not just the software, but the entire infrastructure for product delivery and support.

Proposals

In direct sales software, you may encounter RFPs (requests for proposal) from customers who send their requirements out for bid.

Typically, the sales representative and the systems engineer will respond to this, and a product manager will be directly involved to guide them through the process in many big deals. This is necessary, since the RFP may request information on the product roadmap or require guidance for details that are not readily communicated to the field. In large companies a technical marketing group may be organized to provide this type of field support.

These requests may come at any time, so you cannot schedule time for them. Responses to RFPs often become high priority, since they come with strict deadlines. Seasoned people keep a library of templates, as many RFPs have similar questions.

Even if you have an RFP answer library, it's good to not take these questions for granted! The similarity of some of the questions on various RFPs does not mean they should be answered identically. It's necessary to read each page to understand the nuances. Don't assume something if you do not understand. The sales team is the most familiar with the account, so they can provide additional guidance.

Collateral Documentation

Product management will work with the marketing communications group on collateral documentation. This includes paper datasheets, Web pages, and other methods for communicating on your product. The audience may vary from end-users and CIOs to your own sales staff, or even reviewers of the product. The idea is to not waste time rewriting each one from scratch. I recommend you devise a standard *positioning framework* that states:

❏ Benefits
❏ Supporting points
❏ Examples

Use this statement to create the other collateral documents that are all aligned with the framework.

The benefits of using such a framework are:

❏ Your communication is consistent.

❏ People don't have to become too creative or risk coming up with something that is inconsistent at best and contradictory at worst.

❏ You support a central strategy, corporate goal, etc.

I have seen different groups effectively reinvent the wheel each time in creating collateral or other communications material, while precious hours are wasted on rewrites.

GATHERING REQUIREMENTS

To best understand how to gather the requirements for the software, let's go back to the distinction between software that helps enable sales, and those that are operational in nature.

People who purchase sales enabling software may have difficulty articulating their precise technical requirements because they are not technologists.

They often cannot specify ahead of time precisely what they need, and it requires a lot of skill and experience on the product manager part – and a few iterations – to design the proper product. You will need to get incremental feedback from sales and field support and tech support people, make changes to the specifications, and send it back through data and sales cycles to test the assumptions.

Therefore, you have to go through a lot more give-and-take to fine-tune a sales-related product. A technological utility-type product may not be as flashy, but the people who use it tend to be more technically savvy, so they can articulate precisely what they need. But since they are technical, you may get very precise requirements – and a lot of them. Getting too many requirements is a nice problem to have, though. All you have to do is perform the not so simple task of prioritizing them. That may sound difficult, but it pales in comparison to trying to prioritize vague requirements or not having requirements at all.

It's very easy for your product to become overladen with features, and that is a common problem. As it gets richer, you have the choice of designing the product so that you can streamline it – maybe split off the product into different modules.

Role of Careful Project Management

You cannot neglect the value of good project management – the nitty-gritty details of making sure all the ducks are lined up.

This may be a contentious point, but I think a product manager should set the design goal for a product. It's important that there be a design goal that is accepted by all parties. What do I mean by a design goal? It should be closely tied to the product positioning: Who this is for and what benefits they will get.

If the design goal is loose or nonexistent, everyone will interpret the goals his or her own way. The product may become what sales feels they can sell (and requested that engineering make real), or a product that engineering feels is appropriate, with no real connection to customer needs or demands. People on your production team may squabble because they all have their own ideas about the goals.

Disagreements are natural, but the situation is especially bad when people think they agree on something, when in reality they have different goals based on different interpretations. It's as though a football player has interpreted a coach's play to his own preferences.

There are many analogies. They are basically variants on the theme of "too many cooks spoil the broth."

Imagine a car design team pondering the next sports car. The team members consider how to design or incorporate a sleek shape, a zippy engine, fat and sticky tires, and all the other things that go into a performance car.

Now, let's say you open up the design process to a larger group. It's a good idea to get a lot of people's input, but if taken to its extreme, the results can be disastrous, as I illustrate below.

Let's say your car company has not gotten into the SUV business and has some inkling that it wants to. There are no SUVs in your design pipeline, and many customers are defecting to competitors to buy SUVs.

If you open up the design process to the car dealers, for example, the conversation may go something like this. Let's imagine an open forum where dealers can voice their opinions to the design manager, who fills the role of a product manager in our illustration.

Dealer A: "I'm from the XYZ dealership. A lot of my customers are looking for an SUV, or something that's a little *outdoorsy*. All I have to sell them are these sleek, low-to-the-ground, two-door convertibles. What can we do to make them happy?"

Design Manager: "An SUV? Is that what you want? No can do, at least in the next few years. The development time for an SUV is at least three years, since we have to start from scratch."

Dealer A: "You've got to give me something. We're dying here. My dealership is out by the mountains, and lots of folks want SUVs."

Dealer B: "I don't know, Mr. A. I think the current design is just fine. We sell lots of sports cars."

Dealer A: "Hey, what if we make the current sports car a little tougher, just like those Model XXX from Maker YYY. You know, we can stick these wire protectors on a new set of fog lamps, add some rugged tires, and yeah, let's stick the spare out on the back."

Dealer B: "Umm. You sure about that?"

Design Manager: "We do sell sports cars. I don't think this is the right direction."

Dealer C: "Hey. My customer base is getting old. I think they want more luxury and something more mainstream. Can we put in a cushier suspension?"

Design Manager: "And what? The next thing you know, you'd want a landau roof?"

(Lots of murmuring.)

At the end of the day a spreadsheet-toting finance department, which wanted to maximize the potential sales from all customers, far and wide, overruled the design manager. Lots of strange rumors swirl around in the trade press. Auto magazines whisper about major design changes. A year later, at an auto show, the New *Dirt Sports Coupe* is launched.

Reactions abound. Quotes are instantly lifted by marketing spinmeisters and gingerly placed in the store brochures, just like in movie ads.

"…Interesting experiment…" – Pauline

"Definitely different from before." – Gene

"Who would have thought of this?" – Roger

The result is that all too often, you end up with a product that may be *number two on everyone's list, but number one on nobody's list.*

Although nobody has made a mistake as radical (or absurd) as the one in this story, I think misfortune has befallen many car companies over the years in similar and subtle ways. As you can guess, the formerly premier sports car maker in our little story has been overtaken by the previously also-ran sports car maker, who stuck to its goal of a 100 percent sports car. SUV makers felt at most a tiny bump underneath their tires, since no SUV fan would consider the Dirt Coupe a serious contender to eat into the SUV makers' market share

Let's return to the issue of setting clear goals.

If the goals are properly set, then any mature person can make proper decisions on his or her own, even in times of change or need for rapid decision-making. All you have to do is ask, "How should we act, given our goals?"

You can say this story just couldn't happen in software or in any other industry where products can be measured in an objective manner. After all, likes and dislikes for cars are often emotional and subject to whims of the moment. But there are small aspects that would certainly affect software design. Consider all parts of a software package. Instead of the SUV versus sports car dimension, let's look at two ends of a spectrum that ranges from ease of use to high-function, industrial quality. There are lots of compromises:

❏ User interface: Should there be a menu- or wizard-driven interface that guides people along each step?

❏ Documentation: Should there be a simple, task-based manual that concentrates on most common tasks and how to accomplish them, along with all the details in an online help file, or a hefty manual set that describes all the operations and options in mind-numbing detail?

❏ Support structure: Do-it-yourself support via the Web site, with pay-per-call, or a support contract?

Since software is so flexible, some people are tempted to say: "We can do both! We can put in a wizard *and* a special interface." True, it's possible to do that technically, but there are still a lot of subtle effects. A menu bolted onto a professional-looking tool may alienate some people, or it may make the design cumbersome.

Accountability

Loose leadership creates loose products. In a manner similar to the design goals discussed earlier, it's good to make sure there's an owner for the product and a clean way to make decisions. It doesn't matter where the decision needs to be made. In some companies it goes right to the top. In others it's distributed. People's egos may get in the way, or people may squabble. The main point is that it's better to make a decision than make no decision at all.

Is it better to make one mediocre decision than none? Sometimes it is. You can often claim one bad decision is better than indecision. For example, a company I know of ended up, due to acquisitions, with two parallel software development projects that performed similar functions, aimed at a similar customer base. Each group had a good rationale for continuing with the product. But the result is that, as with this illustration of indecision, you get distracted; resources are diluted; and people end up worried and unhappy.

So let's assume that, all else being equal, one product is better than the other, but that gets canceled. Is that a good thing? Of course not. A good product team gets its project canceled; the team gets disbanded; and a mediocre product gets out to the marketplace. But think about the alternatives. There could have been two failures – two mediocre products that end up failing because of inadequate resources to support them. Two products get canceled; two teams get disbanded; and two products die on the vine.

Resource Planning

Balancing demands from different groups is a common issue where various groups request changes in priority for their own issues, and all the requests seem valid. The lesson in all of this is to be honest and increase trust in the organization.

For example, the technical support group may ask for better quality control to reduce unnecessary support telephone calls. The sales group may ask for changes to make the product flashier to demonstrate, or they may ask for changes in a feature list priority to assist their sales cycle.

In a perfect world you would be able to weigh each request according to the impact it has on revenue. In the real world it becomes an art to balance expectations, reality, and wishful thinking. When a product manager is placed in the middle, listening to all of these requests, it's easy to see the requests as complaints and selfish desires. Instead, it's best to understand the underlying issues that bring those requests to the forefront and comprehend precisely how to weigh those needs in the context of the overall business issues, as opposed to assessing the requests independently.

Sales Expectations

Let's illustrate with a sales representative who states, "If we can add this feature, we can bring in this customer who will sign a $3 million contract." A cynical or suspicious person may say in a knee-jerk reaction, "I think he is overstating that by $1 million. It really is a $2 million sale, so I need to lower the projection." If there is a repeated, consistent pattern, then it may be valid to raise those suspicions, but all too often you don't know. In most cases people do not intentionally lie or intend to deceive. There is misunderstanding, or wishful thinking, and those projections get passed around from person to person until they take on a life of their own and cause confusion.

Perhaps the customer is overstating the potential purchase to get features he needs. "If I can just get feature X, my life will be easier. I can free up some in-house resources and make my next project come under budget." Perhaps the customer himself does not know and is just giving a high-end number to be safe. The dangling of a feature request and the high sales number wasn't coordinated in a concerted way; it just happened that Customer X wanted feature Y, and that Customer X happens to have a budget of $4 million for a certain type of product. The $4 million may be allocated completely to a single vendor, or it can be spread among a set of products slated to deliver a solution. Feature Y may be a desired feature, but it was never slated to be a deal breaker. If clear communication does not occur, feature Y may take a life of its own, as a must-have feature that will bring home the bacon. Is there someone to blame? Most likely not, but having clear communication among sales, systems engineers (SEs), support, and product management will help clear that up. In the long term things tend to clear up. Perhaps inexperienced salespeople communicated incorrectly or didn't correctly size up the opportunity.

Support Needs

Technical support has a different perspective. As with all other stakeholders, they want the firm to succeed, but they typically keep an eye on containing costs. It's true that support can generate revenue through service contracts, but in reality their main goals are to provide customer satisfaction within their limited resources. The real issue here is how to establish a set of goals and an environment where support requests and needs are appropriately viewed to affect the company's success, as opposed to being narrowly defined under "cost containment."

Let's say the support group expends a significant proportion of its efforts to solve initial installation problems. Is that representative of the resources allocated in software development? Certainly a great deal of effort goes into installation, but you need to assess whether installation issues are preventing sales or effective use and deployment. Here are the possible scenarios:

❏ Most people install. Some people do not get into detailed use. So a large number of complaints tend to be about installation.

❏ People are most likely in touch with sales and support during the early stages. During the early stages of use people are installing; therefore you tend to hear more about installation problems.

Do you want to make installation smooth and painless? Ideally, yes, since that is the first impression people have of your product. But look at the higher level and think of the cost and benefit of having your sales support staff on-site to perform the installation. If that happens, the first impression of the customer becomes that of the installed application. But you spent time and money installing the application. Is there a net benefit? I think it's mostly a sales issue, but you can discuss this with your sales and support staff to see if it's a tradeoff you are willing to make.

Project Planning

Managing expectations and lead time is largely a people issue. Some people are eager to please, so they promise Herculean schedules and efforts – then end up missing them and disappointing. You don't want to drag your feet, either, and say you can't deliver – then come up with the results. In a sense, that's underpromising and overdelivering. It's also an issue of honesty. Let everyone expect realistic results, and all parties will be happy.

If you are known to pad your schedules, then people start to count that in. If you start to be inconsistent and pad schedules some of the time and are realistic other times, then you are setting yourself up for failure, since people cannot plan around your expectations.

You Do Your Job, I Do Mine

There's a fine line between butting your head into someone else's job and keeping to yourself too much.

If you are not 100 percent satisfied with some software prototype you are reviewing, you can fly into a fit: "This is no good! I can do better than that. Look at this flub and that mistake. Can't you do better here?"

From a developer's standpoint, you are being completely random. Most engineers are rational, logical, reasonable people. The developer knows you were not involved in the intricate design decisions, the tradeoffs, and the schedule crunch. And most likely you came in at the last moment to critique his work, rather than "taste testing" the soup in the kitchen earlier.

The flip side is complete trust. You stay away from the "artists at work"; you are surprised at the result; and then say to yourself, "I guess that's what I asked for." The engineers see no reactions from you and assume that silence is consent. That's wrong, too.

Be fair and honest, and accept the give and take. If you really care about a product in development, take a look at some intermediate results and make comments.

Ultimately, "That's not my job" is the statement you are slated to eliminate. If details are falling through the cracks, you either have to find someone to deal with it, hire someone new to deal with it, or do it yourself.

PROCESS ORIENTED

VERSUS

MARKET REACTIVE

There are two ways to approach product management. The process-oriented approach is a somewhat linear process, in which you lay out a straight line from product inception to sales, using careful product requirements and design.

The other type is completely reactive to the message the market offers.

You can't take strictly one approach or the other. Here are some reasons why they fail.

Process Oriented

This is the problem of taking the Soviet 10-year-plan as the basis for software development. It sometimes appeals to some kinds of technical people who like to work in a predictable environment. Its appeal is that there is very little effort wasted. What people do not realize, however, is that it may create a product that very few people want or are willing to pay much money for.

Here's the process-oriented ideal. Step by step, you create:

1. A complete understanding of the customer's needs
2. A complete understanding of the market size
3. A complete understanding of the technical feasibility
4. A complete market requirements document
5. A complete product requirements document
6. A complete engineering product feasibility study
7. A complete engineering delivery schedule
8. A perfect beta and product launch plan
9. A perfect prediction of sales revenues, and hence a set of quotas
10. A perfect product launch

You then obtain great product reviews from the press. All sales betas and sales closing move according to plan. Everyone is happy, and you go home on time.

Of course, this never happens. Nobody ever dreams of it; yet some people still treat it as an ideal goal and work toward it. Nobody ever knows what's going on in detail, but people still try to gather data.

But in reality:

Nobody actually knows the market size. Market research firms often try to sell reports of "well-known" market metrics, but they often describe hugely optimistic product adoption.

Sales people don't know the details of the product because the product is still ill-defined, so they cannot gauge customer reaction or demand.

What does this mean? Perhaps it's better to work from loose goals, set some high-level objectives, and then make your team nimble enough to adapt to marketplace changes. I'm not suggesting that high-level goals change, since they need to be fixed ahead of time. I'm suggesting the need for nimble course adjustments, as opposed to major route changes.

Market Reactive

Let's consider the downside to going in the opposite direction.

If you're overly market-reactive, you basically end up becoming a custom programming shop for your customer. Consider the creation a beta or preview edition of your software and having your sales team deliver it for review. The customer asks for some changes; your sales team delivers the message; and the product team responds immediately to meet those needs. Meanwhile, another sales team delivers another set of different requests, and your product team realizes the two sets of requests are mutually exclusive.

It's as though one asks for a pink background for the user interface and another asks for blue. You can't have both, and let's say for the sake of the argument that it's something that can't be easily customized or changed in the field by systems engineers.

What do you do? Do you favor one over the other? That would require prioritizing one customer over another, which often is difficult to do, since the sales manager wants to close both deals.

If your company is indecisive and wants to please everyone, it decides to create, support, and sell both the blue and the pink options. But you if multiply this by a dozen times, the firm effectively becomes a custom-programming house. What drives companies down the path toward excessive customization?

Mismatch of Features

One driving factor is that your product just didn't hit the mark. It may deliver basic inherent, intrinsic value, but it was wrapped in a bad user interface. Since UI is highly subjective, people want them personally appealing. Without a good UI, customers often do not get to appreciate even the fundamental functionality of your product.

If the customers manage to comprehend the product's functionality, but they do not like the interface, then they will ask for customization.

To avoid performing excessive UI customization for each customer, the technical solution may be to design a flexible foundation on which you can layer individualized styles. Or you can create a good software development toolkit (SDK) so that customers customize the product on their own.

Wrong Expectations

If sales or marketing creates a wrong set of expectations, then you can get a large amount of customization requests to fulfill those expectations. Certainly, it's a fine line, since you cannot have a "take it or leave it" attitude.

On the other hand, you don't want the sales force to treat each mismatch of customer expectation and product features as a deal-breaker. In an ideal case you want them to manage the customer's expectations so that:

❏ The customer's requirements were incorporated into the product design.

❏ Marketing and sales clearly communicate how product offerings are aligned with customer's needs.

❏ You make a clear representation of the product's inherent value, as opposed to some wishful thinking of what it offers.

TECHNICAL SOLUTIONS FOR

METHODOLOGIES

It appears that much of product management requires juggling requirements from customers and setting goals and communicating them to the team members. Are there tools or methodologies that enable that? There are some that try to capture the bookkeeping aspects in an automated way.

For requirements management, there are tools such as Rational Software's RequisitePro. But let's see where it makes sense to adopt them, and where it makes sense to have some caution before adopting them wholesale.

Experiment with Tools That Fit

There are countless books on different processes, and they all sound reasonable on the surface. It's best to understand whether or not the tools fit your company's culture. If your company is structured appropriately, or is receptive to new ways of doing things, it may be worth considering bringing in these new tools or methodologies.

But there's danger if the company's work culture is highly resistant. In that case you may need to take things slowly. Some simple guidelines or frameworks, as opposed to detailed development methodologies may be sufficient.

I refer you to the bibliography for various articles.

Extreme Programming

We discussed extreme programming earlier and want to revisit how extreme programming may conflict with classic product management.

When does it make sense to take a great leap and consider a radical process? It would be wise to consider such "out of the box" development methodologies if you find great problems with the existing system, and the organization lends itself to new methods. If there are deeply rooted traditions of classic, linear product management processes, then you will likely find great resistance. That's because extreme programming allows extremely close interactions between product managers (business analysts) and engineers and supports rapid feedback loops, as opposed to extensive planning.

Extreme programming is worth looking at if:

❑ You are unable to get detailed requirements.
❑ You can afford to work with a rapid and incremental development method.
❑ The project is small enough to allow you to experiment.
❑ You are using project management tools.

People who are technical have a tendency to try to manage software products using some automated tools. They believe they can place all tasks into a project management tool (using Pert charts, Gantt charts, etc.) to help them track the process. They realize there is a lot of human interaction involved, but think that such a tool helps keep things smoothly recorded and managed. It stems from an inherent desire to inject orderliness into life.

This sounds good in theory, but in reality software is a complex product to manage, and it resists complete control via software project management tools. Using project management software is great if you are trying to deal with a construction project, contractors, and such, but I feel that software is too complex and unpredictable to deal in this manner, for several reasons.

The items and tasks that go into a project management tool are well-defined items with clear boundaries. Many software tasks are ill-defined and more fluid. Take, for example, the need to write specs or product requirements. The deliverable, such as a spec, seems to be clearly written, but how complete can it be if requirements are still ambiguous? Will it require additional engineering review to make it truly useful? How can you predict how to define a product if it's a new, yet unknown product that's creating a new category of its own?

Software designers, engineers, and others are more likely to resist being treated as building blocks in a mechanical plan. Some consider themselves artists (there's a lot of truth behind that) and resist allowing their schedules to be predicted and planned months ahead of time.

How did Leonardo Da Vinci know when he would complete the *Mona Lisa*? Some people say a product is finished when it's finished!

There needs to be some rigor and structure in any development plan, but I prefer not to work in a group that treats themselves as "PERT chart elements." There needs to be some pride in what they do as a creative endeavor, since it's always good to have people who treat their profession as a craft and who take pride in their work and designs.

AUGMENTING WITH
NEW FEATURES

Augmenting a product with new features can be done in many ways.

In packaged software you'll be doing a whole new release. A version 1.0 product gets revamped as 1.5, and so on. Enabling downloads of enhancements via the Net may give you some leeway with updates, but the basic parts of the product cannot be easily be upgraded.

With a direct sales product, you have a little more flexibility. You have to have rigorously tested versions that are released periodically, but you have the flexibility of sending out special modules that augment or fix small features. They are called patches, field updates, or service packs; we'll use the last term in our discussion.

You don't do a rearchitect of a product in a service pack, but modern systems introduce the flexibility in delivering new features as add-on modules or snap-on products.

Note that in many cases, people get lazy and start to slip new features into a service pack, rather than waiting to release it in a full-fledged release. I feel this is a dangerous trend, since service packs often do not go through a full testing or beta test cycle.

Let's see what happens when you augment a product with new features.

In a brand new product (version 1), you're essentially marketing and producing requirements for the potential end-users and creating a feature set with a blank slate. As with drawing or painting on a blank canvas, this is easy to do, as there is nothing on the canvas to disturb.

When you're augmenting an existing product with an updated version, you now have to balance a lot of different requirements. You have a large set of stakeholders to satisfy – sales, customers, finance, and tech support, for example. And there is an existing customer base, which may have different needs or requirements than the new customers you want to capture.

There are many benefits to having an existing customer base. You now have real, live customers to validate ideas you want to consider for the next release.

The questions are: Are the requirements you had originally for the first release of the product still appropriate for the product as it evolves? Are the first set of customers and their requirements representative of the large pool of customers yet untapped?

You are very lucky if they are aligned, because you have validation that your original product design is correct, and enhancements for the product simply take you down the correct path.

However, if you based your requirements for version 1.0 of the product on a customer set that's a little quirky, you need to make a decision. Should you evolve the product to continue to meet the needs of this quirky customer, or revise your vision for the larger, untapped market?

That's a judgment call you have to make based on the intelligence you have from the field salespeople and your channel partners, and going back to some of the research you did earlier, as well relying on some additional market research.

Gathering Enhancement Requests

If your company has the luxury of running some surveys, you can afford to conduct surveys in a rigorous, quantified way. But startups and small companies may not have the luxury of performing large-scale market research.

Here are some of the things you can do to get information on enhancement requirements.

One is to discuss requirements with your systems engineers, who can tell you precisely what the problems are in the feature set, performance, and installation issues. Then triangulate to find out if there are patterns.

- ❏ Are you losing sales based on critical deficiencies?
- ❏ Are you losing on customer satisfaction, based on unmet needs in the product?
- ❏ Are customer satisfaction issues related to the product, or to issues of the quality of technical support?
- ❏ If the problem is support issues, can you talk to the customer support staff to see what those issues are?

One of the key issues of enhancing a product is tracking where a request came from, and closing the loop. You often forget where an enhancement request came from, so when it's time to actually create detailed requirements and specs, you don't know who to talk to for details.

This type of closed loop also is a great sales tool. You can make the customer very happy because they feel appreciated and recognized. Engineers and designers are also very happy, since they get validation from precisely the person who wanted these features.

Another source of enhancement ideas is the technical writers. Although they don't have direct customer contact, they often receive feedback regarding the documents, which may provide excellent clues regarding problems in usage or understanding the benefits of the product. Since technical writers are an inherently thoughtful group of people, they can analyze this sort of feedback and tell you precisely whether the suggestions are for enhancing the documents or the product. Feedback on documentation may not be a great source of ideas on completely new feature sets, but issues regarding usability and ease of installation are often gleaned from the writing group.

Channel partners may provide an interesting source of enhancements ideas, as well. Their motivations are similar to those of salespeople, and they may provide enhancement suggestions in the same vein as the sales group. But there is an extra twist, since channel partners often augment their revenue stream with value-add services.

If a partner generates a fair amount of revenue from customization or installation services, a channel partner may suggest to the software makers new enhancements that may reduce that extra revenue stream. But if your long-term strategy is to court and recruit channel sales partners, then it's good to know what opportunities to make available for them, so you can create a great long-term partnership.

You have to take things with a grain of salt and understand what kind of software product you have. If you have a product that's more of a platform onto which value-add partners write software, and if you are trying to add features that eat into their business, you have to be very careful: If you add those features, you'll reduce the incentive for the channel partner to sell your product.

End-user suggestions may come from unorthodox sources. User groups are an interesting source of ideas. If resources permit, you can perform a user group tour. You can attend their general meetings and meet the all members, or perhaps arrange a one-to-one interview with their key influential members. The latter may be an inexpensive way to recruit a focus group or a board of advisors. The user-group members are big fans of your software, and they will be more than happy to provide ideas on future versions.

If your firm writes mass-market software, you can take a page from classic brand management and follow an end-user home to see how they use the program, observe the problems they encounter, and casually ask how they want to see improvements. People may be more relaxed at home and more candid about ideas.

You may even make a surprise visit to a retail store and ask potential customers about their buying processes. Are there things that keep people from buying your products? Can you interview the salespeople at the store? Do people clearly understand what the product does? Note that specialized software stores staffed with enthusiasts are rapidly disappearing. Performing this research with salespeople in an office super-store may be a fruitless effort.

Product reviewers in a magazine or on a Web site have a lot of opinions on software. Many online product reviews are augmented with end-user reviews and commentaries.

You need to be careful with unedited reviews, since many comments are anonymous, and they tend to attract many complainers. The complaints of a few people don't necessarily represent or reflect an overall pattern.

Is the Product Failing?

Sometimes, a product does not sell well, and the product manager needs to decide whether to enhance the product in an attempt to revive it, or scrap the product altogether. In either case you need to understand the fundamental causes of failure.

If the competition has developed a product that is superior, then you want to understand precisely what the competition has done and see if you can outdo it.

❏ Is the issue technical?
  ❏ Should you make the installation smoother? Do you need to add more features?
❏ Is the issue sales-related?

❑ Should you change the pricing, the packaging, or the distribution to counter your competitor's channel mix?

If the product does not sell, even if there are no competitors, then you have a different problem altogether.

Your problem could be just a lack of awareness; the product is available, but your target users are not aware of it. That may be a sales, marketing, or distribution problem.

Perhaps the product is ahead of its time. The customers are not acutely aware of problem it is trying to solve – it's fixing a problem that isn't there. Many highly technical products fall into this trap.

After assessing all of the data, you have to step back and consider the basic assumptions that led to the product launch to determine whether you should "can" the software or improve it.

Quite often, companies valiantly hang on to a software product long after its usefulness has leveled off. Product managers may have illusions of demand that's "right around the corner." It's often good to recognize there really is no demand, and the right decision is to cut your losses and go allocate your company resources to something else.

To continue chasing an illusionary market is ultimately a sad exercise, not just for the product manager, but for everyone else on the team, too – whether they're developing, selling, or promoting the software.

You slowly come upon a realization that there is no inherent demand, but people sometimes go into denial even in the face of mounting evidence. Eventually, the truth will catch up, and morale goes down.

Rather than feeling defeat, this may be a time to perform a post-mortem analysis to determine whether the assumptions behind the product at its inception were fundamentally wrong, or it's simply a matter of timing.

Timing is an often neglected issue. You may have gathered marketing requirements appropriate for 2003, and if your product takes a year longer to develop, the market may have changed sufficiently that you have missed the window. It may be for technical reasons (compatibility with other software) or missing a technical transition wave (client-server versus Web-based computing, for example).

There's always a bit of luck involved in predicting the future. Nobody has a perfect crystal ball, so the next best thing is to be aware of the industry dynamics and noting the directions in which people are going. As Wayne Gretsky, a famous hockey player, once said, you succeed because you skate to where the puck is going to be.

Hindsight provides perfect insight. Many people are known to say, "I saw that trend and thought of this product ten years ago!" In reality technical trends are extremely difficult to predict. I admit luck has a lot to do with it.

There's always a risk and reward tradeoff in product management. If you are superconservative, you'll never have a great success, since the products you create will be based only on the tried and true. If you want to create some new category of software, you are a risk-taker who is willing to make a bet.

It's like a roulette wheel. The odds are high, and the payoff is big. But if you bet only on black or red, then you can be relatively certain of what you'll get.

SOFTWARE LOCALIZATION

If you intend to develop products for the international market, these products must be localized to different national languages. There are several things that must be considered, two of which are:

❑ The actual language of the text (with its character sets and character encoding)

❑ The use of culturally specific examples that might not translate well from one language or culture to the next, such as sports analogies. A baseball analogy may work well in America and Japan, but in other countries it would simply not make sense. They probably prefer to play soccer instead.

One of the biggest mistakes that companies make when they attempt to localize a product is that they either completely ignore the issue and focus mainly on the United States, or they fall on the opposite end of the spectrum and assume their product will be completely localized from the beginning, even though their market demand may not be there. The latter situation causes a delay in the marketing of the product even for the home market, because a localized product takes longer to prepare.

The most pragmatic thing to do is to make general accommodations within the software, including the *ability* to accommodate different languages *in the future,* but not necessarily spending all of the time localizing the text.

Technically, this means UNICODE-enabling the software and ensuring that all of the text strings are separated, so they can be changed without recompiling the main source code.

Interestingly, a lot of international customers are quite satisfied using the English version of the software. The reasons for this are:

❏ Customers are quite conversant in English (especially the technical software people who must read most instructions in English).

❏ Most U.S. firms making software release patches and fixes in U.S. English first, and since many customers always want the latest software fixes, they choose to run the U.S. edition.

Nevertheless, there are many cases where localization is indeed necessary. For example, you might be selling to international government organizations, and there may be a mandate in place stating the software must be localized. There is obviously no way to avoid this.

It all boils down to being careful about your demand, your market opportunity, and the customers who will be using your product. If you create a piece of software that is highly technical and will be used by primarily English-speaking people, you may be able to get away with not localizing as early as with other software.

Many people assume you can localize software by simply "throwing it over the fence," to a localization group within your company or an outsourced localization company. What are the differences in using internal resource versus an outsourcer?

If you ask an outsourced firm to localize version 1 of your software, and then later return to have version 2 localized, you may encounter a *different* staff working on version 2. The reason is that many of the outsourcing companies outsource their work as well.

In this situation you face the problems of having to teach the outsourced team the subtleties of your technologies, and the specific terminology of your software to a different team each time you hire a localization outsourcer. This is obviously not as efficient as having a continuous team available to you.

If you have permanent localization staff in your company, they might be completely familiar with all of the subtleties of the software and more able to get up to speed quickly. The downside is that most of this staff is not required for all 12 months of the year, so it seems to be a waste of money to retain them (unless they can do other jobs in your company).

Localization teams are usually needed for the big push immediately *after* the English release, when the English version serves as a foundation for each localized version. A good compromise is to hire some permanent staff who are extremely familiar with your software and hire outsourcers to fill in the gaps when there is a big push. A larger software company that is constantly releasing different software pieces can more easily justify having localization staff inside the company.

Software Viability in the International Market

When sizing up international market opportunities, you must do the same type of work that would be done in developing a domestic marketing scenario. This entails identifying the strengths and weaknesses of your product in that particular market.

You must also look at your product's strengths and weaknesses in the context of what type of competition you plan to have in each market.

For example, if you are going to write word-processing software, there is a significant chance you'll have some local competition, since word processing is highly language specific.

If this competition has an extremely strong foothold, it may be difficult for you to penetrate that market from scratch. The other issue in competition comes from threats of any company, existing or up-and-coming, that may come out with a range of similar products that could easily expand into your space. These are all common things you must consider.

Cost is another consideration in introducing your software on an international level. It is not as simple as creating and localizing your software in the U.S. and then shipping and selling it internationally. You must address all of the support and sales implications. Although fundamentally it is no different from doing analysis for a U.S.-based product, you must consider all of the subtleties that are involved in doing things internationally – the motivations for people in different countries to purchase a product and how you can sustain that in the long term.

Some people enter an international market, even while knowing it will be a loss in the short term, to keep another competitor out and to carve out a presence while waiting for the market to develop.

The differences in penetrating the various markets in separate countries must truly be examined on a case-by-case basis. For technical reasons, sometimes it is easier for a U.S.-based company to enter a European market because of the similarities in the character sets. But European markets may also host many local (and international) competitors. Asia (with the exception of Japan), Africa, and the Middle East currently do not have a large software industry.

Another issue to consider is writing software for a particular platform, whether it is Unix, Macintosh, or Windows PC. In the past France had a stronger leaning toward the Apple Macintosh than the rest of the European countries, although such differences are starting to gradually disappear. I suspect that Linux adoption may increase in the long term, especially in countries that are very cost conscious.

Copyright Issues From Country to Country

Piracy is more prevalent outside of the U.S. If your software has loose copyright protection schemes, there is a good chance it will get pirated when you enter the international markets. It may be prudent to examine copy protection in international versions, even if your U.S. edition does not incorporate strong copy-protection schemes.

The most extreme case in the past has involved dongles, which are boxes that connect to the I/O port PC that perform as enabling keys for software. People generally do not like them because they are very cumbersome to deal with. With the increased adoption of network connectivity, the use of activation keys is starting to become popular, which reversed a decades-old transition away from copy protection locks within the U.S., so it may be possible to impose a uniform copy protection scheme worldwide. But in general, piracy is extremely difficult to defeat.

Perhaps a separate issue is to consider the rationale for piracy. Corporate piracy tends to be due to risk aversion issues. It's easy to become a victim of a corporate piracy audit, and the penalties and negative publicity impose a high cost. Yet, piracy does occur within corporations. It occurs not because people are being malicious, but because people who are deploying copies may not be completely aware of what the purchasing department has negotiated with the company. So they may accidentally deploy extra copies and *effectively* end up pirating. In those cases licensing keys or licensing servers provide you with the ability to gently nudge the end-user into reminding themselves to rework their licensing agreement if they deploy to more users than originally agreed upon.

Country-specific Barriers

Sales channel issues often manifest themselves internationally, and you must be careful if the sales model will affect product design and content.

In Japan for example, enterprise customers are accustomed to purchasing systems integration services along with the hardware from hardware makers, such as Hitachi. Unlike the U.S., hardware makers hold a bigger share of this integration business. The customers look to the hardware makers to help them choose and install the systems, and the relationship may extend into the management of the systems themselves. This situation is not unlike how customers may purchase services form IBM Global Services, along with hardware from IBM.

The implication of this for a product manager is that gaining entry into such a country with strong influence of the hardware makers may require you to create alliances with the hardware makers early on. The secondary effect is that your software may not be required to provide some type of close integration with the hardware – perhaps it is support for a peripheral, or a complementary software product they sell.

BUSINESS DEVELOPMENT

AND PARTNERSHIPS

Business development and partnerships are not strictly a part of product management, but there are lots of areas in which the two groups collaborate.

There's always a tension regarding when you want to create a partnership to assist in the technical development of your product or to create a new sales channel. Some issues of contention are:

When to Start These Discussions

It's always difficult to determine the perfect time to approach a partner. Different parties want to introduce the product early for different reasons. Let's examine what the problems would be in each case.

Too Early

Some people are just too eager to introduce their product to potential partners. They may have little else to do, so they want to get something going.

There's a danger of hiring staff for these projects too early, or getting too enthusiastic about it. Some of the dangers are:

❏ The product is too immature; it looks rough. The partners can't see the technical parts, since you see a rough UI. They can laugh you out of the office, and you don't get a second chance because you lost credibility.

❏ The partners ask for detailed technical information, and your so-called partners end up copying the product or introducing a product or create an initiative to position themselves as a credible competitor. This happens when a partner may be potential competitor. Unless you have patent protection or an ironclad nondisclosure agreement, preventing ideas from being misappropriated is very difficult.

❏ The product information leaks out to potential customers who choose not to buy the current product and to wait for the new edition. This is bad if you are already selling one version of a product and are still months away from a version upgrade cycle. There are many examples in the industry where news leaks about a new product cause the current sales revenues to dry up. I think one of the earliest and most famous such occurrence was with Osborne Computers, one of the earliest portable PC makers, which leaked information regarding a new model. Its sales declined rapidly, and the company eventually went out of business.

In the software industry people are getting clever about ways to control this problem. They often include some type of upgrade guarantee if people buy within a certain period. If you plan (and you better meet this schedule!) to release a new edition on January 1, you create a special promotion period from October 1 to December 31. Customers who purchase the old product during this period can get the new version free upon its release.

That offer is supposed to get the sales to continue moving smoothly without a sudden dip. In reality it's not a perfect solution, since most customers (especially in commercial accounts) do not want to deploy an old version, only to turn around and install a new version a few months later. But this may work for retail sales products, or to somehow capture commercial accounts that need to spend money before a fiscal year ends, so they can get delivery of the new product in the new fiscal year.

Too Late

You become too cautious and wait too long before creating partnerships. Perhaps you waited until the product is almost ready to ship. Here some things that may happen.

❑ A competitor materializes, and quietly they forge a partnership with your potential partner before you do, and you are locked out.

❑ You lose a short window where your product is considered interesting. As sad as it may seem, some products and technologies follow the winds of fashion, and although your product may still offer inherent value, it may no longer be fashionable. So if you miss that opportunity, your partner may no longer find you fashionable enough to talk to. (This may work in reverse, as well, where you may be early, and the idea is not yet in fashion.)

What's In It For Me?

The basic thing to think about in partnerships is: "What's in it for the partner?" They don't really care about how cool the product is or how profitable it is for *you*. All they want is to make sure it helps them reach *their* goals. (This goes back to the chapter discussing motivations.)

In making presentations that tout your product, make sure you include the following information:

❏ Who are the common customers? Is your customer their customer too? If the customer is happy, you both benefit.

❏ What's preventing your partner from making sales? Can you be a catalyst?

❏ Can you be a complement? Sometimes, you present something that accidentally eats into the partner's product line. Don't do that. If it does, downplay it.

PRACTICAL POINTERS AND

MANAGEMENT MYTHS

Practical Pointers

Here is a grab-bag of different ideas and hints, based on experiences and actual circumstances product managers encounter in real life.

Methodology du Jour

Just as management consultants come up with new theories for new books every few years, software experts create new software development methodologies.

Software development methodologies (related to writing code) do not affect product management directly, but in reality we see a great overlap in the gray areas of specification, requirements analysis, incremental release cycles, and other aspects that lie between product management and development.

Take extreme programming, which we discussed earlier. As a caveat, please note that I did not participate in an XP project, so I do not have firsthand experience. But here are some ramifications of this development methodology on product management, based on general knowledge I have, as well as discussions I've participated in about its merits.

One of the basic lessons of XP is to have rapid and incremental changes to the software and specs. You do not create a detailed spec, but instead you create numerous incremental releases rapidly, learn from them, and then cycle back.

This technique flies in the face of classic product management, so there are people who feel religiously both for it and against it. In the XP philosophy you either buy it 100 percent, or you don't use it. So an attempt to merge XP with traditional product management in a halfway point technique is bound to fail, since the basic assumptions are radically different.

But let's believe for a moment that your team is having problems in the development process. The development staff and the product management staff have agreed that an experiment is in order to see if you can improve the process. You say, "Perhaps rapid, incremental development is the answer."

Someone writes a general spec, and engineering starts to develop the software. But you discover that the early results do not fit the user requirements. End-users reject the early prototypes. The end-users can't clearly state what is wrong or why it's wrong. But they know that what they see is not what they want.

What happened here? One problem was that end-users were not able to adequately describe their needs to the product manager. You wrote an early spec based on vague or incomplete requirements and presented that to the engineering group. You convinced yourself that the XP style of development will be able to recover any problems of ambiguity, since you can quickly recover and rewrite the code. Development just followed your spec and created something that didn't fit the bill.

You recognize the mistake you made, but you console yourself: "Since I now have an incremental, rapid development methodology, I know I can satisfy all parties by exploiting the rapid turnaround I get." You believe you can use XP as a crutch for the inadequate requirements-gathering you performed.

I think you did not step back and think about what went wrong in the first iteration. You didn't manage to get the right requirements, so you did not get the right spec written, and, accordingly, the wrong functional spec got generated.

You have to ask the right questions before jumping into XP, and this may apply to adopting any new magic bullet that is proposed to you. I'm sure many consultants are willing to present new approaches, and there are great case studies presented at conferences to draw from, but ultimately you are the one who decides what you need to do. That decision needs to be based on your overall business goals: You need to determine whether the benefits of a particular methodology are aligned with the business you are in. If your product is the creation of a software program that tries to address very vague or unclear end-user requirements, then a rapid-development methodology may make sense. If you are creating a technical product where the needs are clearly known ahead of time, then the benefits of an incremental development methodology become less clear.

Testing My Understanding

This is a great lesson I learned from a quality-training course I took many years ago.

The basic instructions are: When you hear someone say something, you repeat it, but restate it in your own words. You don't want to just parrot their words. You restate it to verify that you understood what was said. For example, let's look as a contrived conversation.

Customer: "I want a drink."
You: "You said: 'I want a drink.'"

Your response doesn't help, since it just repeats the phrase. What you want to do is to clarify.

Customer: "I want a drink."

You: "Let me test my understanding. You want some beverage because you are thirsty."

Now we're getting someplace.

Customer: "I'm not thirsty. I need a stiff drink. I've had a hard day, and I could use a shot of whiskey."

Hmm, now it's a different matter. Joking aside, you can use this technique to clarify. If you do it too much, you sound like an idiot who can't understand what anyone's saying. Use it whenever you suspect there may be some misunderstanding. Specifically, use it to sift out vague requests or high-level requests. Here's a more realistic sample conversation:

Customer: "My app seems too slow."

You: "To test my understanding: Your app doesn't give you answers quick enough."

Customer: "No, the answers are quick. The user interface is sluggish, so I can't get it to accept my input parameters efficiently. The choice menu takes a long time to display because the end-users are frequently on a slow dialup."

You: "I see. The back end is fast enough. You want a faster front end to let you drive the app more efficiently."

Customer: "Exactly."

Supercomplex Frameworks

Product managers who have a technical background often create a really complex framework to gather end-user requirements. For example, let's say you are collecting end-user requirements to create a marketing requirement document. Some product managers get caught up in the process, or the "cool" tools that enable them to do their job.

They may create a complex description of end-user preferences, plot them onto different axes of preferences, generate fancy graphs in PowerPoint presentations, run numeric analysis end-user types, run numbers to find clusters, and end up with a 200-page research document and a 100-page marketing requirements document.

There may be cases when that complexity is useful, but in reality nobody really understands it. It's not that they are stupid. It's most likely that they don't have the time; for the majority of the audience the stuff is so esoteric it loses their interest. The process is not the important part, and everyone needs to keep an eye on the concrete goal: Is it useful for the reader?

The key thing to do is to find out the audience. If the reader is a busy executive who needs to read the summary and approve, then make sure you write a clear, crisp executive summary, and then support the information in an appendix with proper data to back it up.

If the readers are a group of technical people, then you take a different approach. In addition to all the information you provided the executive, you may need to emphasize such technical aspects as performance and platform compatibility.

Management Myths

Let's discuss come common delusions that can lead a product manager down the wrong path.

"One customer bought it; everyone must like it."

This delusion goes back to the problem of finding a perfect customer profile. If you substitute a persona for a set of statistics, then you can put a face on it and rally around that as the ideal customer. It works; it's fun to personify abstract market data; and it's easy to develop an emotional attachment to it.

It is a useful tool. But as with many good things, it's easy to go overboard and extrapolate. Remember that the synthetic persona is a combination of many statistics. It's designed to put a face on an average user, and it's useful during the design process. You can start to use this technique after a product ships by becoming overly chummy with one live-customer.

Just because one customer states a need for some particular feature, you can't assume that most people will share the same opinion. Despite an overwhelming need to talk to more customers to validate some assumptions, since you are chummy with this special customer, you convince yourself that the idea is true and become unwilling to validate your assumptions through talking with more customers.

I'm not saying that you must go out and talk to ten thousand people to get a good sample. It's just not good to base your perception of your market's size on the beliefs of that one friend.

"Nobody's buying; there must be no market."

This is the reverse of the previous delusion. The absence of a product from the marketplace does not mean there is no need, and therefore no market, for your new product. Logically speaking, there is always someone who is first to market, so you might as well be the first one.

Predetermined market research categories often reinforce these misconceptions. In trying to determine market size you read some market research and find a few market segments that are somewhat close to your proposed product. You proclaim that you are going after a $100 million market. Or you get discouraged, since nobody has defined a market segment for your proposed product, so there is a zero market opportunity.

If you are creating a special widget, and the market research company's reports list only five traditional categories, and your widget does not fit into any of them, does that mean there is no market? Absolutely not.

You have to base your market and product strategy on unmet needs, rather than needs that are already met. This is the reason the ideas for many successful products are based on a deep understanding of needs augmented by some lucky hunches, and not based on pure market research numbers alone.

"There are no other solutions."

This delusion is analyzing a customer need and giving up on creating a solution because a single competitor has filled that need. There's always more than one solution to a problem, so having a potential competitor should not discourage you. You cannot be totally risk-averse, and there is some suspension of disbelief necessary to make the jump to create a product.

"Someone else did it, so we must do it, too."

This mistake is closely related to the previous mistake – but it leads to a "me too" product. Unless you have some overwhelming advantage, such as a sales or distribution channel, a tie-in to an existing product, or a technical advantage, a me-too product is positioned for failure. Rather than creating an alternative solution, you simply create the same solution. I suspect this, too, is a case of risk-aversion raising its ugly head. Rather than trying to innovate, you take the safe route taken by someone else.

The route may be large enough for one party. The resulting competitors end up trying to differentiate themselves, but this often leads to unhappy confusion. They discover there are few ways to differentiate other than price, leading to a price war, where all parties lose. Or they try to position themselves based on some petty differences.

Obviously, you must learn from the characteristics that make the competitor successful, and perhaps copy them. There are also often some basic baselines a product must uniquely possess.

Why does this mistake happen so often? It's a form of self-deception. You hear from customers a need for some product to fill an unmet need. That does not necessarily mean that such a product does not exist. It's just that this customer is unaware of such an existing product, or your competitor ran a poor sales campaign.

Your first reaction is to convince yourself a need exists for product X. That's fine. But then you do something odd. You start looking for potential competitors and realize that some companies do exist. You also find out they are making money (or have raised money, or have earned some measure of success or attention). This discovery then leads to a belief that you, too, can make money, since there is a huge unmet demand.

The problems are obvious. There is a competitor, so unless you differentiate in some substantive way, you just end up going head-to-head.

Your potential customer's stated desire for such a product doesn't necessarily mean they are truly willing to buy the product. It's dangerous to overextrapolate. Here, you need a fair amount of common sense and pragmatic thinking, but a problem that may occur is that you actually hear from several other customers that they do not want or need such a product. But at that time you start to wear selective blinders on your ideas, so you listen only to things you want to hear.

I raise this rather obvious point, since this is bound to occur frequently in our world of increased commoditization.

Many fallacies can draw people in. Some people convince themselves the product is a commodity, but they can win by a lower price, or a lower cost structure than competitors. But I'd bet that many others are singing the same tune.

"There's a spreadsheet, so it must be right."

People often create spreadsheets to justify market size, market demand, or market opportunities. You can justify almost anything in a spreadsheet. For some inexplicable reason, people may disbelieve oral arguments or words on paper, but some people tend to believe in spreadsheet analysis. Perhaps the problem is some deep fear of numbers, which leads to a irrational trust of them.

Look what spreadsheets have gotten us into.

❑ *Dot-coms:* The business will become profitable when 200 million people become customers. And, by the way, it costs $200 to acquire each customer, but the spreadsheet shows that as the idea scales to 90 percent of the world population, we will break even.

❏ *Savings-and-loan debacle:* We created scores of buildings that stood empty for years. The real estate debacle no doubt had greed driving its source, but it was fueled by spreadsheet-based justification.

❏ *A trillion-dollar market size for PDAs:* Enough said.

If someone wants you to sell an idea, and back it up with some numbers, you can always construct a spreadsheet with some vague numbers, multiplied by unreliable numbers, resulting in some unsubstantiated numbers known as the "recommendation." By analyzing the basic assumptions, rather than the formulas on the spreadsheet, it's easy to unearth some clear misconceptions.

TECHNOLOGY TRENDS –

AND A BIT OF HISTORY

Let's look at some broad trends to help you design a roadmap to create products for customers whose needs may constantly evolve.

We'll first take a brief look at some history – and note some disconnected trends that came together, producing some *unintended consequences*. Fans of James Burke's books and television show, *Connections,* in the early 1980s may find this line of reasoning somewhat familiar.

Many years ago, before Unix systems were used in business, most people used IBM mainframes and other large systems from Burroughs, Sperry-Univac, NCR, Control Data, Honeywell, and others. They were mostly based on proprietary technology; their product life cycles were long; and the technology base was stable.

Starting in the late 1960s and into the 1970s, minicomputers become popular. They were first used in scientific computing. The premier maker was Digital Equipment Corporation, which produced popular the PDP-11 series minicomputers, which were mostly used in technical areas. From that base they created the VAX-11 series of computers that helped gradually garner business accounts.

But the origins of Digital Equipment Corporation were rooted in scientific computing, and it was an ideal system for academic computing and research labs.

The primary operating system on the VAX was the VMS operating system, but an interesting consequence was that the PDP-11 and VAX computers also became the test-bed for the Unix operating system, mostly because the DEC computers offered good price and performance, and were purchased heavily by universities and research laboratories, which were heavily instrumental in developing the Unix operating system. Other computers had parts of the Unix OS, but PDP-11 and VAXs almost became the reference systems where Unix ran.

One university with particularly strong ties to Unix development was UC Berkeley, which had a project in its Computer Systems Research Group, sponsored by the

Defense Advanced Projects Agency (DARPA). This group had a project that resulted in modifications of the Bell Labs' Unix system and the creation of a version of Unix that added the use virtual memory for the VAX systems, a TCP/IP network stack, and a fast file system, among other features. This version of Unix was released as the Berkeley Software Distribution, which was distributed on tape, along with the source code.

Although the goals of the project were not to freely share code, another unintended consequence was that it got many people accustomed to the idea of seeing and sharing source code, making modifications and improvements, and sharing it with the community. This sort of collaboration was rarely seen in other operating systems. People did share code in user groups and in some specialized research operating systems, but Unix created a common, standard platform that truly achieved critical mass.

The rapid adoption of TCP/IP networking in academia, along with the adoption of the USENET newsgroups, and of course, the widespread use of e-mail, helped this trend.

Although the original Bell Labs Unix source code was protected, the numerous improvements made by students and staff of UC Berkeley and other places were not copyrighted by Bell Labs, so those pieces of source code were widely distributed, shared, and modified. Eventually, a subculture was created where new pieces of code that were unrelated to the original Unix system became a "must-have" set of Unix applications, and were widely shared and worked on. At the same time, Bell Labs made additional improvements to Unix, such as in System V, as well as research versions of Unix, but they did not find widespread acceptance in academia.

Meanwhile, another innovative force in the early to mid-1980s was the GNU project, whose original goal was to create a Unix-compatible system (GNU stands for GNU's Not Unix), but its most famous early legacy was the popularization of Richard Stallman's EMACS editor (which was originally popular on a previous generation of DEC systems), and the compiler tools such as the GNU C Compiler and other tools that benefited from a large army of dedicated – and altruistic – engineers who created first-class tools to be shared by the greater community. The source was shared in the community via the GNU General Public License (GPL) sometimes referred to as *copyleft*, to distinguish it from the more common *copyright*.

The subculture of sharing code and the widespread availability of source code that had Berkeley Unix as the catalyst set the foundation that enabled projects such as GNU to prosper.

All this happened before the term *open-source* came into vogue, and before Linux and Apache and other popular forces of the 1990s made open-source all the rage.

Let's now look at what was happening on the hardware side of the world.

As students familiar with Unix systems graduated and went to work in industry, they wanted to create commercial systems that ran on the operating systems they were familiar with. Furthermore, since Unix was highly portable (not highly dependent on a particular CPU architecture), it was the first and only choice to port Unix to a new range of systems that came into being with good price performance in the early 1980s.

It did not make sense to create a new operating system to match new hardware. If you created a new "box" based on the then popular Motorola 68000 series of processors, it just made sense to make a Unix port. You received immediate access to plenty of utility software and a readily trained army of new graduates. Most important, it enabled these hardware makers to gain access to applications software.

Certainly, companies tried to create a new platform with their own proprietary software. The first company was Three Rivers Computer Company, an offshoot of Carnegie-Mellon University. They created a workstation system called Perq, which was inspired by Xerox PARC technology.

Apollo Computers was another company with similar goals. This company originated from engineers at Prime computer, a competitor of DEC. Apollo had great software ambitions, which led to the creation of a distributed workstation system with its own proprietary operating system.

A quick retrace of the events so far:

Digital made computers that were used by both Bell Labs and by a group of government-sponsored computer programmers in a premier engineering school. Although the software itself was great accomplishment, it unleashed the forces that led to the ability to create low-cost, high-performance hardware systems that ran the Unix operating system. People got accustomed to the idea of sharing source code, ranging from the basic underpinnings, such as the operating system, through the utilities.

All of this did not occur in a vacuum. It also depended on the availability of reasonably fast CPUs from companies such as Motorola, with its 68000 series of microprocessors, the gradual decline in memory prices, and the availability of high-performance and low-cost disk drives.

Many companies took advantage of this convergence. Many workstation vendors chose to use standard CPUs. Some companies decided to create VAX substitutes by designing their own CPUs. But in general they all ran some variant of the Unix operating system.

This group of companies includes many that we have almost forgotten today, such as Ridge Computers and MassComp. Many companies took a workstation design from Stanford University and commercialized it. Although there were many, the foremost – and the only major survivor – was Sun Microsystems.

As Unix systems became more popular in the late 1980s, DEC gradually got pushed aside and started to lose market share. It declined and was eventually absorbed and compacted by Compaq Computer.

Now, let's focus on the item that's most relevant for this discussion and rather long train of thought.

Because of the trends that DEC *unleashed* many years earlier, Unix systems became popular in scientific and technical computing. After many years business software, such as relational databases, also became available on Unix.

DEC competitors were able to thrive by offering an alternative platform to DEC's VAX systems, with better price and performance. By standardizing on Unix, customers were able to experiment on a wide variety of the hardware that offered better performance, since they were not locked into VAX or VMS.

As people gravitated to Unix systems for technical computing, Digital Equipment started to lose in the technical marketplace, its traditional stronghold.

But DEC did not worry, as it was starting to pull in revenue on the business side of computing, and DEC basked in the knowledge that people finally believed it was a viable alternative to IBM. DEC executives probably thought,

"Why compete on price in technical computing, when we can make money on business systems?"

But companies such as Sun were not concentrating solely on technical computing. Sun, along with Hewlett-Packard (which later merged with Compaq, the company that purchased DEC, along with Tandem), used Unix as a platform from which to create a viable hardware business for all sorts of computing – technical, as well as business computing.

The whole reason for this discussion was not to talk about the demise of DEC or the rise of Sun. The purpose is to point out the chain of events and elements that caused the rise of an open, popular, and standardized computing platform. This was no longer the world of the mainframes and proprietary minicomputers. Unix enabled higher degrees of standardization and interoperability and ports of software.

Various independent forces allowed Unix to become popular (Berkeley, popularity of the DEC hardware platform in scientific and computing circles). The popularity of such a platform made possible the sharing of software within a larger community, through the Berkeley Software Distribution first, and later through GNU, Linux, and Apache. The most noteworthy of these is Linux, but there are other variants such as Free BSD and NetBSD.

So several divergent forces converged to almost commoditize a certain computing niche. Certainly, one can accuse Solaris and HP-UX to be quasiproprietary, but in the grand scheme of things, it is nowhere near as proprietary as what CDC systems or IBM systems had.

Some of you may be wondering, "Where's Microsoft, Cisco, and Intel in this story?" They were extremely important in computing, but practically speaking, they were not critical to the early stages of evolution of this particular branch of computing, which I believe will become highly influential in our future. They were, of course, highly influential in what was to come in the next few years in this story.

What we now have are the foundations of fairly inexpensive software and the germs of a new business idea of open-source computing, in which:

❏ People pay really next to nothing for the software.
❏ There is a fair amount of altruism in writing code for sharing and for fun.
❏ Companies that choose to make money in open source community plan to generate revenue from providing services, as well as from software license fees.

Whether or not you agree with their philosophy is not the issue here. It's more interesting to consider the long-term implications.

Now, let's tie the rise of Unix into another completely separate branch of computing evolution.

Around the same time a lot of people were thinking, from a technical software engineering point of view, "It would be nice if software programs could talk to each other because they could rely on stable and fixed interfaces." It never happened because people said, "Standards are nice, but unfortunately we have too many standards." Early de jure standards were often not widely adopted.

But over the years Unix systems and other open systems became much better at interoperating with each other. Previous generations of systems from disparate vendors like IBM AS/400, DEC VAX VMS, and Apollo workstations never shared data easily.

Why did Unix systems communicate with each other well? Berkeley-derived Unix systems spoke TCP/IP and ran on similar programming interfaces (such as Unix sockets) that allowed programmers to write portable application code.

Although Unix systems communicated among a variety of different vendors, and communication was easier than making old-fashioned incompatible mainframes talk to each other, it wasn't as easy as a unified set of systems such as:

❏ The old "plug compatible" machines in the IBM mainframe world

❏ The single, proprietary, but compatible range of VAX VMS

❏ (More important) The newly emergent Microsoft/Intel-based systems that were not only source-code compatible, but were completely binary compatible – very much in the same way that IBM or VMS systems were

Unix systems still had something to be desired. People sought binary compatibility in the Unix world, but mostly failed. There were attempts to create an architecture-neutral distribution format (ANDF) allowing "last-minute conversion" of the portable distribution format into binary code, but that didn't catch on.

Earlier similar attempts included the UCSD p-code system that created a virtual machine, where platform-independent code was executed by an interpreter on each target computer. But that was mostly sold on personal computers or workstations and did not catch on for server systems.

People sort of "gave up" on the notion of a perfectly binary-compatible system and relied on having a system ported to each flavor of Unix, which resulted in the Sun Solaris version of the software, or an HP-UX version.

In reality, having a few Unix versions of software was acceptable, since there was consolidation in the Unix hardware and software areas. In the early days there were many variants of Unix on workstations, minicomputers, and mini supercomputers. We had a wide range of operating systems from makers such as Alliant, Convex, ELXSI, Sequent Dynix, Encore, Ridge's ROS, IBM's AIX, DEC (which had its own variant of Unix called Ultrix), MasPar, Convex, and others.

Within a few years the world of Unix had shrunk to a few players, so it was considered manageable for software makers to support a few versions – primarily Solaris, HP-UX, or AIX.

But people knew it was always nicer to have a single binary-compatible architecture. This was just for software distribution reasons, but as systems became complex, people desired fewer "moving parts," and it was understood that a perfectly orchestrated environment is possible only where the many parts work together from the beginning. So one solution was to create a total Solaris environment or a total AIX environment.

This leads us into the next story. Let's review what has happened so far.

Various accidents in computing history lead us to the popularity of Unix, and the seeds of open-source code were dropped into the world, thanks again to Unix and the culture of shared source code initiated by UC Berkeley. The popularity of Unix, however, led to many incompatible variants, which frustrated people who wanted true binary compatibility.

At the same time (in another branch of evolution), in a parallel universe, the Microsoft-Intel based systems were having great success, driven by volume pricing, highly standardized hardware and software, and economies of scale. That universe was growing rapidly, and the two parallel universes were bound to collide.

The Microsoft-Intel computing platform that resulted has these characteristics:

❑ Raised on the desktop, was able to benefit from an open hardware (but not software) platform that created great economies of scale and choice in hardware

❑ All more or less compatible in hardware (disregard the IBM Microchannel versus EISA wars of the early days); the hardware platform is pretty much standardized now, thanks to Intel and Microsoft's guidance in creating reference designs

❑ A *binary*-compatible architecture (remember how this was a secret benefit that VAX/VMS or even a total Solaris environment benefited from)

❑ Gradual growth from the desktop into servers

Note that history was repeating itself. The same characteristics of better price and performance:

❏ Threatened IBM when mainframes became popular

❏ Threatened DEC later when Unix systems became popular

❏ Threatened Unix workstations and servers, by the rise of the PC platform

As Unix people were bickering over the years and were unable to create a single compatible platform, the PC platform has sneaked up from the low end, and its previously toy-like architecture grew up and became a viable server and business computing platform.

A small digression to an interesting side note: The operating system that drove the adoption of PC-based servers into the business world was managed by an ex-Digital Equipment engineer who was originally instrumental in the development of the VMS operating system.

Let's step back and consider the landscape:

❏ PCs are ascendant.

❏ Unix is growing, but beginning to stall.

❏ The technology landscape is beginning to experience ever-faster changes.

❏ The Unix world and the PC world are beginning to collide.

❏ The Unix world is being threatened by the PC world's economies of scale.

Trends come and go and maddening speeds. The issues we discussed earlier, such as different Unix systems, became unimportant. Some trends were short-lived, such as the rise of the interactive television world, which disappeared as quickly as it arrived.

Internet-based networks (not Internet e-commerce, but communications) were not a short-term trend. They were a strong, fundamental force owing their existence to the TCP/IP networking that Berkeley's BSD enabled, later popularized under Unix workstations, and eventually embraced by the PC platforms and the computing industry as a whole (and enabling the rise of Cisco).

Now, let's look at one particular company that behaved like a cat with nine lives – Sun Microsystems. It dodged a bullet when its workstation business became threatened by PCs, and it moved toward selling server systems. It dabbled in different technologies, such as interactive television, but its core business became the business-oriented server system.

As Sun saw greater and greater threats from Microsoft, Sun decided to create a new method of unifying computing – to create a language and an overall computing architecture that allows systems to interoperate over the Net. Much of this was centered on Java. It looks like a clean story, but things didn't start this way. I think it started as an accident, since the origin of Java came from a desire to create a hardware platform for interactive television.

Let's look at what Sun did by looking at the assets it had:

❑ In its advanced development labs, Sun discovered it had developed Java, a reasonably modern language, which is platform independent. There was nothing technically revolutionary about Java, but people liked it, and Sun had the clout to popularize it.

❏ Sun espoused an open platform (its earlier motto was "Open Systems for Open Minds"), but was really tied to its own Sparc CPU architecture and its own Unix variant called Solaris. Its business was an interesting twist on the old DEC VAX business model. (VAX/VMS was compatible from the desktop to the data center. Replace VAX/VMS with Sparc/Solaris and you have the Sun story.)

❏ Sun saw a great threat from Microsoft and Intel. (This is the *key* point here.) Sun, unlike many companies that failed in history, realized it needed to innovate to thrive and create an alternative standard.

The result: Propose Java as the foundation for a platform that can counter Microsoft and Intel, and basically try to forestall or perhaps beat back the fate that had befallen many of Sun's forebears, such as DEC.

The elements started to gel, and Sun began making Java an open standard that was to some extent given away, so it created an industry of people writing software in the Java framework. It's true that Java had some strict licensing requirements (which Microsoft soon discovered), but in general Java was open enough that companies as diverse as IBM started to embrace it.

Looking at this history, note that the manner in which the Java language was made freely available, with its reference implementations, was inspired partially by the pioneering work done elsewhere in the early Unix days with the Berkeley software distributions. Naturally, the specifics of licensing terms are different, but it's somewhat unusual to see a core piece of technology, such as the Java computing platform, so freely shared with a wide group of vendors. Compare that to another "grand unification" software scheme, such as SAA – the Systems Applications Architecture that IBM proposed in the late 1970s, which was highly proprietary.

Before Sun started to evangelize Java, other things were happening in the PC world. Microsoft and Intel platforms continued to evolve to become much more stable. It was no longer based on DOS or Windows (which, as an operating system, can barely be categorized with "real" operating systems). Windows NT was finally a "real" operating system. It was beginning to be deployed into the enterprise because of an increased perception that it was an industrial-strength offering.

Microsoft started to offer an architecture that was just as comprehensive as those that traditional systems vendors had tried to offer. IBM had its Systems Applications Architecture, or SAA, and Digital had its Digital Network Architecture, or DNA. So Microsoft also saw a need to create a unified platform to lock its customers into. It went through various names – WOSA, the Windows Open Systems Architecture, Windows DNA, and other names that marketing created, but the basic characteristics were:

❏ A published set of Windows APIs, so that Windows systems could run in true business applications

❏ A whole framework of underlying supporting pieces to choose from, with support for databases, middleware, and other elements required for serious computing

Sun no doubt looked those developments and thought Java should have the same thing. In reality, I'm sure Sun saw a need for unifying architecture long before that, but at least in the naming and marketing spin it created, we see a pattern in which Sun tried to do a "one to one" on Microsoft's efforts. For example, "Microsoft had ODBC (Open Data Base Connectivity); there should be a Java version of database connectivity called JDBC."

As Sun saw a great threat from the PC world, it basically wanted to extend Java from a simple language into a general computing platform that was an alternative to the growing Microsoft/Windows programming set. So, for each technical component within Windows, there was an analogous counterpart within Java.

Over time the Java platform became comprehensive and was slowly becoming an alternative to the Microsoft platform for programmers and IT professionals who did not want to be locked into a Microsoft environment, did not want to rely on legacy systems, and wanted to move to the future.

Let us elaborate on this and put it in context.

Whereas the Microsoft-Intel platform was tied to the PC architecture, Java took a different route. People began to realize they could employ Java on top of not just Unix, but also PCs, mainframes, and any kind of minisystem. Java and its surrounding computing architecture, such as RMI (Remote Method Invocation), became the glue by which networked, or distributed computing, architecture became a reality on a variety of platforms. It worked, of course, on Sun's platforms, but also on other platforms Java ran on, such as IBM's (AIX as well as mainframes), HP-UX, and others.

Sun made a fair amount of money on hardware, since people perceived that it was the right place to buy a leading-edge solution. But in reality, Java was a reasonable system to run on many other non-Sun systems (including Microsoft's Windows).

Java was initially targeted toward making interactive applications (due to its "write one, run everywhere" philosophy), but in reality it became most important in the server systems that formed the back end of many Internet servers that served Web pages, supporting databases, and the multitiered logic that made it all work. This, I believe was a consequence that was not planned by the original framers of the Java language.

So now all these things started coming into place:

1. DEC enabled Unix to come into fruition.
2. Unix enabled open source and shared code, with great contributions from Berkeley.
3. Unix succeeded, but had a fractured family tree of slightly incompatible systems.
4. Microsoft-Intel succeeded on another branch of the computing evolutionary tree, and started to encroach on Unix (which had already ceded its workstation origins to the PCs and then retreated to a server-based computing platform).
5. The Internet became ubiquitous, thanks largely to the early work done in the Berkeley BSD TCP/IP network stack and the Web later on.

6. Java became popular as a network computing technology. Originally intended to be a browser technology, it ended up becoming a server technology through its J2EE platform.

As separate and disparate as these things seem, all of these trends are related to one another, and each item had a role in enabling the next steps in the story.

Now, a few things that seem unrelated began to happen. They owe part of their existence to the earlier events listed above. Those early stages set in motion a chain of events. At each stage technical innovation allowed for the standardization of lower levels of the technology stack, creating forces that led to the demise of major technology vendors.

Long-term trends in standardized computing from Unix and the Microsoft-Intel front, further enabled by the popularity of TCP/IP networking, somehow encouraged Sun to push for the adoption of Java. Java started as a programming language but later became a platform for network computing. As strange as it may seem, Sun's reaction to the threat of standardized computing was yet another standardized computing platform. Although it worked for a while, I think it set the stage for another cycle of commoditization, as we'll see later on.

Although Java was seen as an open, inexpensive platform, it still enabled some companies to thrive by writing enterprise-class Java (J2EE) software. But other companies did make a fair amount of money on it, notably BEA with WebLogic and IBM with WebSphere. Sun itself did not capitalize on the J2EE software front, but was content to sell its hardware.

Now we begin what I think is the current chapter in this long story. Sun creates an open computing platform to counter the PC juggernaut. It thinks it has created a reasonable counterattack, but I think it will encounter yet another stage of unintended consequences that will set into motion another round of changes in the technology industry.

The technology Sun created to counter the Microsoft-Intel works will have absolutely no problems running on the PC platform, and the "buzz" that Sun relied on to sustain its server sales may find its home in very inexpensive PC-based systems. But I think these PCs may not necessarily be running Microsoft operating systems all the time.

Let's examine this line of thought.

In reaction to the high prices charged for commercial J2EE software, and as a logical consequence of earlier open-source software, we now see various J2EE systems being created and sold at low prices. Since Java (not just J2EE) has created a new lingua franca and accelerated the amount of standardization, people are rapidly creating a whole new class of computing infrastructure, in much the same way that the early days of Berkeley Unix saw the proliferation of many Unix-based utilities and application programs.

This class of software, including J2EE software, such as JBoss; software development testing tools, such as JUnit; and inexpensive source code control systems, all started to become available. In a strange sense the spirit of open-source projects such as GNU has manifested itself within the Java community. But rather than being on the fringe, as GNU was for many years, I feel this type of development is being seriously adopted, even for production systems, at a rapid rate. Traditionally, people would be reluctant to work with such "nonmainstream" software, but I believe they began to realize that many of these Java-derived systems work quite well together.

Is this an unintended result of the commitment of Sun's Java community to create a tight standard? Or is it the result of the collective single-mindedness of the very large open-source community? Who knows? But much of the chaos that characterized early attempts at cross-platform computing doesn't seem to occur here. Although I am aware that people still complain about incompatibilities of various Java Virtual Machines, this time around things are not that bad. People saw that the Microsoft Windows environment worked well together, since it was controlled by one company. But now, as an alternative, J2EE and other related Java technologies, working disparate hardware systems, were working together.

And it's not just between Unix systems, but PCs, mainframes, and other systems, as well. The emphasis here is that it works on inexpensive PCs – the hardware system that Sun was concerned with.

What are the driving factors? Some of them were the standardized Java interfaces that were "good enough." They may not be completely rock solid, but they were "good enough" as an alternative to Microsoft, and with reasonable effort, the collection of Java-based systems were working well enough for the technical members of industry.

So Java, which owes its existence to a Sun, a company that owes its existence to Unix, has enabled a style of computing that allows much interoperability. Its popularity was accelerated by a fair amount of code-sharing. This alternate world is not purely a Java world. It has many products that owe their existence to the open-source world and that collectively create the glue that makes all of these technologies work together. This includes such systems as PHP, Apache, Perl, Python, MySQL, Postgres, and countless others. As diverse as all these systems are, the collective efforts of the countless programmers are beginning to make many of these things work. Those in the know may complain that many items do not work seamlessly, but given how diverse these systems are, the result is a stunning achievement.

So now the puzzling big question is: "If you were a big enterprise that had to run big, mission-critical enterprise computing that just couldn't afford to crash, could you run it on free software?"

At first guess, the obvious answer is "no." Why would people bet the farm on free software? Nobody owns it, so you cannot rely on someone to support it.

In reality, many engineers are quite happy running open-source software. It started to enter into IT organizations through the back door, and even through the front door due to endorsements from firms such as IBM, which, of all companies, started to endorse Linux and Java. Surprisingly, a lot of people claimed that some open-source software was more stable than some purchased software from traditional software companies. Over a few years people began to seriously consider running Linux for computing.

Let's see what this all means.

❏ The cost of computing platforms has decreased drastically.

❏ The software, which was inspired by the Java and Unix world, has become very inexpensive.

❏ The Unix world has spawned the inexpensive software, but the software runs on inexpensive PCs.

❏ The hardware that can run the inexpensive new software was spawned by the Microsoft-Intel world, but the hardware may become increasingly less dependent on Microsoft software.

In the long term, we may see a world where:

❑ Development tools are free or inexpensive.

❑ Platforms are almost free.

❑ Middleware, such as application servers and Web servers, are becoming increasingly cheaper or even free.

And let's not discount Microsoft. Microsoft is aggressively marketing its own Internet platforms. It gives away a Web server with each copy of Windows, and it will aggressively push the .NET platform onto each server and desktop it sells.

In any case, we have cheaper computing platforms and increased levels of commoditization.

We are almost at the end of our story, but now we need to tie it to the topic of product management.

We now have low-cost hardware based on the PC platform and low-cost software based on open-source code. Even if people do not use these systems in the cheapest and purest forms *(e.g.,* running Linux on top of no-name brand PC), *we cannot deny that the availability of inexpensive alternative platforms puts a downward pressure on price.* I think that is the most important point here. Companies will find it harder and harder to develop, market, and sell infrastructure software.

We must realize the *trend* is toward lower prices for many critical components of the infrastructure. There is certainly a pressure toward lowering prices. Even such firms as Oracle see that their least expensive platforms are perceived to be "good enough" for most uses, so people are less likely to purchase their high-end databases.

Will this trend continue? Will everything become more commoditized? How does this affect software product management?

In the beginning everything was not commoditized, but the trend was increasing levels of commoditization from the bottom up. OSs and platforms were the first items to become commoditized. Certainly, companies such as Intel and Microsoft captured the lion's share of the value, and a lot of companies were being pushed aside. People made money selling items higher on the food chain, such as databases (consider Oracle) and application servers (such as BEA), and ERP and CRM software (Siebel, PeopleSoft).

Then tools and utilities slowly started to encroach on the higher parts of the food chain. This is occurring in areas such as database (encroachment from MySQL and Postgres). Let me make a rather foolish extrapolation and assume that some software that's higher than the database will slowly get eaten away either by the "open-source" origin software or even by parts that Microsoft creates.

So now the question is, as a lot more things become commoditized, where do you make money?

❑ What must a product manager think about to evolve products or to create new products?
❑ Will services become increasingly important? Will high value occur in systems integration or customizing software?

❑ Will novel concepts, such as software as a service, take hold?

❑ Will value be created higher in the food chain? We already see success in CRM and ERP companies such as Siebel, PeopleSoft, and SAP. But what if the underlying bases of CRM and ERP systems get standardized, so that parts of these engines become commoditized?

❑ Do you create business that kind of coexists with commoditized software? Perhaps you can provide services, or develop specialized add-ons?

IMPLICATIONS FOR

SUCCESS AND FAILURE

IN SOFTWARE

PRODUCT MANAGEMENT

Our history lesson wasn't meant to portend some singular vision of the future. No one knows what will happen, but in using 20/20 hindsight, I think we can learn what not to do. If we can learn what to avoid, we can probably make a good case for sensible decisions in the future. The following are some lessons from this history.

Don't Get Nostalgic

Even though our mini history lesson may make some people nostalgic about the good old days of computing, the main lesson is that changes can wipe out whole categories of business. People may have felt comfortable, or secure, in DEC, Sun, or IBM – till they saw great changes sweep through and surprise them. It's better to be prepared than to be surprised.

If a company is strong or resilient, it can bounce back. If it does not have enough resourcefulness, it cannot bounce back. A product manager can assist corporate leadership by seeing and identifying trends and by trying to enable change. Don't resist change. Work with the change and be innovative.

See Real Trends, Not False Trends

Seeing actual trends and recognizing them as such is extremely difficult. In retrospect, interactive TV was a false trend. The Internet, regardless of the recent boom and bust, is a fundamental technology that will continue to pervade. The Internet style of computing, ranging from the low-level TCP/IP protocol up through Web protocols, such as HTTP and SOAP, is enabling and modifying the way people interact with computing systems (i.e., the decline of traditional client-server systems and the rise of Web front ends as the primary interaction medium for most back-end systems).

I think the critical thing is to always look at basics: Does it make long-term business sense? How does it fit into the overarching technology trends? For example, you can create your own theories about technology trends and make that a framework in which to pose your questions.

Is the trend toward low-end, commodity hardware and software inevitable? If you believe in it, then make that a singular focus and plan, and place your bet accordingly. Don't make a plan that is halfway there. If you believe, for instance, that low-cost software will wipe out most competitors except your company's, then you'd better have a great reason to believe it.

Move Forward With Your Vision

If you believe you can still continue to thrive in the face of these changes, then either you are in denial, or you work for some incredibly resourceful company that has a great track record for bouncing back.

Halfway beliefs are not a great way to make bets. You need to create a theme and a coherent strategy. If the elements are not cohesive, the actions and your execution of the plan will not be consistent. People will not see a pattern and will be unable to make good independent decisions.

This "lesson" ties back into earlier lessons about having a vision that is consistent. Some may argue that this is a high-risk and high-payoff strategy. It's true, but I claim that a low-risk strategy may end in failure if this results in a company or a team that cannot create and seek a clear goal.

Avoid Complacency

Resting on your laurels can obviously cause long-term problems. Success is often attributable to luck as much as effort and talent, but it's easy for people to believe their talents are solely responsible for their success.

If a product sells well, a person may be led to believe, "I have the magic potion, and I'll continue developing and selling the product just the way I always have and ignore what my competitors are doing."

Such an attitude is obviously flawed but surprisingly common. Combined with inertia, as well as a bit of laziness, it can mold a product management group into relative complacency. I think success tends to be a drug that can warp perceptions.

Regardless of a product's success or failure, you still need to perform a post-mortem evaluation to find out *what* made your product succeed or fail.

If it was weak on features, but you did an incredible job promoting it or gathering sales leads, understand you may not be able to repeat your success each time if a competitor manages to launch a good promotion.

If a great review from a magazine or some well-known newspaper reviewer who writes about technology gave you that push this quarter, realize that glow will fade, and competitors may hone in on features they lack and incorporate them into their product.

Stay Your Course...

You have to know how to compete on your true merits. There is danger if you continuously fine-tune on tactical elements, not paying attention to some of the core things you ought to do.

In sailing, if you want to head in a certain direction, you set sail, knowing the wind will change a little but generally blow from one direction. You then create a high-level strategy for your course, knowing when you will tack, but not making wholesale changes in your course.

Some people may detect the slightest change in the wind and overcompensate or change course and try to catch a better wind elsewhere. If you do that too much, you spend half the time adjusting and not moving forward to where you want to go.

The vision for your product should set your strategy and your course. It's worthwhile to reexamine the vision once in a while, but you don't want to always question the fundamentals, since that will be distracting.

If you're revisiting the core fundamentals about the product, you'll get nowhere and end up sailing in circles. If you wake up one morning and say, "I'm not going after big enterprises; I'm going after small business," what are the implications for this impulsive decision? You need to change your sales strategy, pricing, and even the product documentation. This sudden change causes strain in your marketing and sales, and your revenue either stalls or goes down. So a couple of months later you react: "That small business strategy didn't work. Let's sell to the biggest Fortune 100s and build up a direct sales force."

A few of these rapid changes will end up causing chaos in the organization. The people, their motivations, their attitudes, the processes in place, financial controls, and nearly everything else will be making 180-degree turns.

Once you start questioning assumptions, then people may be paralyzed. "If I take this action, they're going to change it later, so maybe I shouldn't do this at all. Maybe the wind will shift back to where I am, so I should stay still." They start questioning everything you say, and you lose credibility.

Naturally, these wide-ranging decisions are company-wide or divisionwide directions the CEO or division product unit manager or business unit manager has to make, but a product manager is often responsible for part of the answer and can provide great input into these decisions.

…But Remain Flexible

On the other hand, being too stubborn about keeping a steady course will hurt if there are fundamental changes afoot, where you could be caught off guard.

Several years ago, when Unix workstations were hot, people wrote software products that were geared toward that marketplace. You could have gotten caught short if you ignored the rise of Intel and Windows-based PCs that displaced workstations. Initially PCs could not compete with workstations. They were certainly cheaper, but they had less power and less functionality. As time went by, though, they became powerful through hardware advances, and the operating system software caught up to Unix. So what was once a toy started to compete against the high-end workstations that had produced Apollo and Sun. Apollo was absorbed by HP, and Sun effectively became a server company.

For Individuals

A) Establish Your Own Electronic/Print Library

Receive access to hundreds of books and articles already published by Aspatore, or just books and articles in your specialty area, with new publications added every month, to create the ultimate reference library for you to speak intelligently with anyone, in any industry, on any topic. Aspatore publishes approximately 60-70 new books every year, in addition to hundreds of articles, briefings, essays and other publications. Our clients use this information to understand the ever-changing needs of their current clients and industries and to learn about current issues facing their potential customer base. For the electronic library, content can be viewed online, printed, copy and pasted into any PDA, and emailed. Immediately receive access to titles already published (see title list on following pages for titles already published).

i. Electronic Library – Access to Publications in 1 Area Only (Select from: Technology, Legal, Entrepreneurial/Venture Capital, Marketing/Advertising/PR, Management/Consulting, Health, Reference) (Via Password Protected Web Site) - $19.95/Month (1 Quarter Minimum)
ii. Electronic Library – Access to All Publications - $29.95/Month (1 Quarter Minimum)
iii. Print Publications (All Future Publications, Sent as They are Published)-$1,490 a Year
iv. Print Books - (65 Best Sellers Already Published by Aspatore) - $1,089 (A savings of 45%)

B) Your Own Custom Book Every Quarter

Receive 4 quarterly books, each with content from all new books, essays and other Aspatore publications that fit your specialty area. The content is from over 100 publications (books, essays, journals, briefs) published every quarter on various industries, positions, and topics, and available to you months before the general public. Each custom book ranges between 180-280 pages and is based on your Business Intelligence Profile (the one page questionnaire you fill out describing the type of information you are seeking that is in the business reply envelope). You can even put your name on the front cover and give your books a title (ABC Company, Technology Reference Library), although this is optional. Build your own library of custom books with information you are specifically looking for, while saving countless hours of reading and researching, and arm yourself with C-Level business intelligence.
$99 a Quarter or $349 a Year (Books arrive within two weeks of the start of each quarter)

C) PIA (Personal Intelligence Agent) – Custom Reading Lists

Your quarterly PIA report presents you with information on exactly where to find other business intelligence from newly published books, articles, speeches, journals, magazines, web sites and over 30,000 other business intelligence sources (from every major business publisher in the world) that match your business intelligence profile (the one page questionnaire you fill out describing the type of information you are seeking that is in the business reply envelope). Each 8-10 page report looks like a personalized research report and features sections on the most important new books, articles, and speeches to read, one-sentence descriptions of each, approximate reading times and page counts, and information on the author and publication sources - so you can decide what you should read and how to spend your time most efficiently.
$99 a Year for 4 Reports/Year (Reports arrive within two weeks of start of each quarter.)

To Order, Please Call 1-866-Aspatore (277-2867) Or Fill in Order Form & Business Intelligence Profile (in Envelope) & Mail or Fax

For Businesses

A) <u>Establish Your Own Electronic/Print Library</u>

Receive print or electronic access to hundreds of books and articles already published by Aspatore, with new publications added every month, creating the ultimate reference library and enabling your employees to speak intelligently with anyone, in any industry, on any topic. This collection will enable you or anyone on your team to get up to speed quickly on a topic, increasing your chances to close more business, identify new areas for business and speak more intelligently with current and prospective clients. Aspatore publishes approximately 60-70 new books every year, in addition to hundreds of articles, briefings, essays and other publications. Every year, Aspatore publishes C-Level executives from over half the Global 500, chair level executives/lawyers from over half the 100 largest law firms and consulting firms, and leading executives in almost every major industry. Simply subscribe to the entire library or books and other publications published only in one area of interest, or make your electronic library available to customers as a resource for them as well. For the electronic library, content can be viewed online, printed, copy and pasted into any PDA, and emailed. To see sample main navigation page, please visit www.aspatore.com/elibrary4.asp.

Titles in Your Industry Only

i. Electronic access to publications in your company's specialty area/area or industry that you sell your products/services to (Select from: Technology, Legal, Entrepreneurial/Venture Capital, Marketing/Advertising/PR, Management/ Consulting, Health, Reference) (Via Password Protected Web Site) - For examples of titles that would be made available immediately, see sample titles page.
Pricing - $499 a month (1 Quarter Minimum), $399 a month (1 Year Minimum), $249 a month (5 Year Minimum), Price includes up to 50 user seats (individuals that can access the site, both employees and customers), Each additional seat is $25 a month

Access to All Titles

ii) Electronic access to receive every publication published by Aspatore a year. Approximately 60-70 books a year, hundreds of other publications and 50+ best selling books on the sample books page (on the following pages) made available immediately.
Pricing - $999 a month (1 Quarter Minimum), $899 a month (1 Year Minimum), $699 a month (5 Year Minimum), Price includes up to 50 user seats (individuals that can access the site, both employees and customers), Each additional seat is $35 a month

Access to All Titles With Additional Navigation

iii) Same as ii, however all publications are arranged by different divisions of your company, each with its own web site. Upon order, you will receive an email from our editors about setting up a time to discuss navigation for your business.
Pricing - $1999 a month (1 Quarter Minimum), $1799 a month (1 Year Minimum), $1399 a month (5 Year Minimum), Price includes up to 100 overall user seats and up to 10 different web sites, Each additional seat is $45 a month

iv) Print Publications (All Future Publications Sent as They are Published)-$1,490 a Year

v) Print Books-Build Your Own Corporate Library (65 Best Sellers Already Published by Aspatore) - $1,089 (A savings of 45%)

To Order, Please Call 1-8<u>66</u>-Aspatore (277-2867) Or Fill in Order Form & Business Intelligence Profile (in Envelope) & Mail or Fax

B) <u>Your Own Company Book Every Quarter</u>

Receive 4 quarterly books, each with content from all new books, essays and other publications by Aspatore during the quarter that fits your area of specialty. The content is from over 100 publications (books, essays, journals, briefs) published every quarter on various industries, positions, and topics, available to you months before the general public. Each custom book ranges between 180-280 pages and is based on your company's Business Intelligence Profile. Up to 50 pages of text can be added in each book, enabling you to customize the book for particular practice groups, teams, new hires or even clients. Put your company name on the front cover and give your books a title (ABC Technology, Technology Reference Library), if you like.

Please call 1-866-Aspatore (277-2867) or visit www.Aspatore.com for pricing

C) <u>PIA (Personal Intelligence Agent) – Custom Company Reading Lists</u>

Corporate PIA Reports present your entire company, or a division/group within a company, with information on exactly where to find additional business intelligence from newly published books, articles, speeches, journals, magazines, web sites and over 30,000 other business intelligence sources (from every major business publisher in the world) that match your business intelligence. Each 8-10 page report features sections on the most important new books, articles, and speeches to read, one-sentence descriptions of each, approximate reading times and page counts, and information on the author and publication sources - so you can decide what you should read and how to spend your time most efficiently.

For 1 Report For Entire Company, $499 a Year for 4 Quarterly Reports, Copies Permitted (Reports arrive within two weeks of start of each quarter.)

For Multiple Reports For Same Company, Please call 1-866-Aspatore (277-2867)

D) <u>License Content Published by Aspatore</u>

For information on licensing content published by Aspatore for a web site, corporate intranet, extranet, newsletter, direct mail, book or in any other way, please email store@aspatore.com.

E) <u>Bulk Orders of Books & Chapter Excerpts</u>

For information on bulk purchases of books or chapter excerpts (specific chapters within a book, bound as their own mini-book), please email store@aspatore.com. For orders over 100 books or chapter excerpts, company logos and additional text can be added to the book. Use for sales and marketing, direct mail and trade show work.

Business Intelligence Profile

Please fill in answers on the page in the envelope.

Your Business Intelligence Profile is Based On:

1. The amount of time you have to spend on reading and analyzing business intelligence every quarter
2. Information you are looking for on your area of specialization and/or industry
3. Your preferred type of business media (books, speeches, magazines, newspapers, Web sites, journals, white papers)
4. Business information most relevant to you (e.g., articles on your industry in a particular periodical)

Sample Questions

Please fill in answers on the page in the envelope.

A: What industries should your PIA report cover (such as auto, technology, venture capital, real estate, advertising, etc.)?

B: What area of specialty should your PIA report cover (such as technology, marketing, management, legal, financial, business development)?

C: What level are you at in your career (entry level, manager, VP, CFO, COO, CTO, CMO CEO, etc.) ?

D: What is your preferred source for business intelligence (books, magazines, newspapers, journals, web sites, speeches, interviews)?

E: Are there any particular publications your PIA report should specifically cover (such as The Wall Street Journal, Business Week, books published by Aspatore, etc.)?

F: How many hours do you spend reading business intelligence (books, articles, speeches, interviews) every week? Every month?

G: How many books are you comfortable reading every quarter?

H: Are there any key terms or concepts you are looking to stay on top of (such as nanotechnology, business-to-business marketing, online privacy, etc.)?

I: Is there any other information your PIA should know in order to better customize your quarterly report?

To Order, Please Call 1-8<u>66</u>-Aspatore (277-2867) Or Fill in Order Form & Business Intelligence Profile (in Envelope) & Mail or Fax

Praise for Aspatore

"What C-Level executives read to keep their edge and make pivotal business decisions. Timeless classics for indispensable knowledge." - Richard Costello, Manager-Corporate Marketing, General Electric

"True insight from the doers in the industry, as opposed to the critics on the sideline." - Steve Hanson, CEO, On Semiconductor

"Unlike any other business books…captures the essence, the deep-down thinking processes, of people who make things happen." - Martin Cooper, CEO, Arraycomm

"The only useful way to get so many good minds speaking on a complex topic." - Scott Bradner, Senior Technical Consultant, Harvard University

"Easy, insightful reading that can't be found anywhere else." - Domenick Esposito, Vice Chairman, BDO Seidman

"A rare peek behind the curtains and into the minds of the industry's best." - Brandon Baum, Partner, Cooley Godward

"Intensely personal, practical advice from seasoned dealmakers." - Mary Ann Jorgenson, Business Chair, Squire, Sanders & Dempsey

"Become an expert yourself by learning from experts." Jennifer Openshaw, Founder, Women's Financial Network, Inc.

"Real advice from real experts that improves your game immediately." - Dan Woods, CTO, Capital Thinking

"Get real cutting edge industry insight from executives who are on the front lines." - Bob Gemmell, CEO, Digital Wireless

"An unprecedented collection of best practices and insight..." - Mike Toma, CTO, eLabor

"Must have information for business executives." - Alex Wilmerding, Principal, Boston Capital Ventures

"An important read for those who want to gain insight....lifetimes of knowledge and understanding..." - Anthony Russo, Ph.D., CEO, Noonan Russo Communications

"A tremendous treasure trove of knowledge...perfect for the novice or the seasoned veteran."- Thomas Amberg, CEO, Cushman Amberg Comm.

"A wealth of real world experience from the industry leaders you can use in your own business." - Doug Cavit, CTO, McAfee.com

Sample Books
(Also Available Individually At Your Local Bookstore)

MANAGEMENT/CONSULTING

Empower Profits –The Secrets to Cutting Costs & Making Money in ANY Economy
Building an Empire-The 10 Most Important Concepts to Focus a Business on the Way to Dominating the Business World
Leading CEOs-CEOs Reveal the Secrets to Leadership & Profiting in Any Economy
Leading Consultants - Industry Leaders Share Their Knowledge on the Art of Consulting
Recession Profiteers- How to Profit in a Recession & Wipe Out the Competition
Managing & Profiting in a Down Economy – Leading CEOs Reveal the Secrets to Increased Profits and Success in a Turbulent Economy
Leading Women-What It Takes to Succeed & Have It All in the 21st Century
Management & Leadership-How to Get There, Stay There, and Empower Others
Human Resources & Building a Winning Team-Retaining Employees & Leadership
Become a CEO-The Golden Rules to Rising the Ranks of Leadership
Leading Deal Makers-Leveraging Your Position and the Art of Deal Making
The Art of Deal Making-The Secrets to the Deal Making Process
Management Consulting Brainstormers – Question Blocks & Idea Worksheets

TECHNOLOGY

Leading CTOs-Leading CTOs Reveal the Secrets to the Art, Science & Future of Technology
Software Product Management-Managing Software Development from Idea to Development to Marketing to Sales
The Wireless Industry-Leading CEOs Share Their Knowledge on The Future of the Wireless Revolution
Know What the CTO Knows - The Tricks of the Trade and Ways for Anyone to Understand the Language of the Techies
Web 2.0 – The Future of the Internet and Technology Economy
The Semiconductor Industry-Leading CEOs Share Their Knowledge on the Future of Semiconductors
Techie Talk- The Tricks of the Trade and Ways to Develop, Implement and Capitalize on the Best Technologies in the World
Technology Brainstormers – Question Blocks & Idea Development Worksheets

VENTURE CAPITAL/ENTREPRENEURIAL

Term Sheets & Valuations-A Detailed Look at the Intricacies of Term Sheets & Valuations
Deal Terms- The Finer Points of Deal Structures, Valuations, Term Sheets, Stock Options and Getting Deals Done
Leading Deal Makers-Leveraging Your Position and the Art of Deal Making
The Art of Deal Making-The Secrets to the Deal Making Process
Hunting Venture Capital-Understanding the VC Process and Capturing an Investment
The Golden Rules of Venture Capitalists –Valuing Companies, Identifying Opportunities, Detecting Trends, Term Sheets and Valuations
Entrepreneurial Momentum- Gaining Traction for Businesses of All Sizes to Take the Step to the Next Level
The Entrepreneurial Problem Solver- Entrepreneurial Strategies for Identifying Opportunities in the Marketplace
Entrepreneurial Brainstormers – Question Blocks & Idea Development Worksheets

To Order, Please Call 1-866-Aspatore (277-2867) Or Fill in Order Form & Business Intelligence Profile (in Envelope) & Mail or Fax

LEGAL

Privacy Matters – Leading Privacy Visionaries Share Their Knowledge on How Privacy on the Internet Will Affect Everyone

Leading Lawyers – Legal Visionaries Share Their Knowledge on the Future Legal Issues That Will Shape Our World

Leading Labor Lawyers-Labor Chairs Reveal the Secrets to the Art & Science of Labor Law

Leading Litigators-Litigation Chairs Revel the Secrets to the Art & Science of Litigation

Leading IP Lawyers-IP Chairs Reveal the Secrets to the Art & Science of IP Law

Leading Patent Lawyers –The & Science of Patent Law

Internet Lawyers-Important Answers to Issues For Every Entrepreneur, Lawyer & Anyone With a Web Site

Legal Brainstormers – Question Blocks & Idea Development Worksheets

FINANCIAL

Textbook Finance - The Fundamentals We Should All Know (And Remember) About Finance

Know What the CFO Knows - Leading CFOs Reveal What the Rest of Us Should Know About the Financial Side of Companies

Leading Accountants-The Golden Rules of Accounting & the Future of the Accounting Industry and Profession

Leading Investment Bankers-Leading I-Bankers Reveal the Secrets to the Art & Science of Investment Banking

The Financial Services Industry-The Future of the Financial Services Industry & Professions

MARKETING/ADVERTISING/PR

Leading Marketers-Leading Chief Marketing Officers Reveal the Secrets to Building a Billion Dollar Brand

Emphatic Marketing-Getting the World to Notice and Use Your Company

Leading Advertisers-Advertising CEOs Reveal the Tricks of the Advertising Profession

The Art of PR-Leading PR CEOs Reveal the Secrets to the Public Relations Profession

The Art of Building a Brand –The Secrets to Building Brands

The Golden Rules of Marketing – Leading Marketers Reveal the Secrets to Marketing, Advertising and Building Successful Brands

PR Visionaries-The Golden Rules of PR

Textbook Marketing - The Fundamentals We Should All Know (And Remember) About Marketing

Know What the VP of Marketing Knows –What Everyone Should Know About Marketing, For the Rest of Us Not in Marketing

Marketing Brainstormers – Question Blocks & Idea Development Worksheets

Guerrilla Marketing-The Best of Guerrilla Marketing-Big Marketing Ideas For a Small Budget

The Art of Sales - The Secrets for Anyone to Become a Rainmaker and Why Everyone in a Company Should be a Salesperson

The Art of Customer Service –The Secrets to Lifetime Customers, Clients and Employees Through Impeccable Customer Service

REFERENCE

ExecRecs- Executive Recommendations For The Best Products, Services & Intelligence Executives Use to Excel

The Business Translator-Business Words, Phrases & Customs in Over 90 Languages

Well Read-The Reference for Must Read Business Books & More...

Business Travel Bible (BTB) – Must Have Information for Business Travelers

Business Grammar, Style & Usage-Rules for Articulate and Polished Business Writing

and Speaking

To Order, Please Call 1-866-Aspatore (277-2867) Or Fill in Order Form & Business Intelligence Profile (in Envelope) & Mail or Fax

A Brief Bibliography

Leffingwell, Dean, and Widrig, Don. *Managing Software Requirements: A Unified Approach*. Boston, MA: Addison-Wesley Publishing Company, 2001. ISBN 0-20161-593-2. A detailed book on understanding requirements and creating specifications. Written by developers of Rationale Software Corporation's RequisitePro requirements management software, it advocates that product's view of case analysis and design models. Even if you do not use this software product, the lessons will still be useful.

McConnell, Steve. *Software Project Survival Guide*. Redmond, WA: Microsoft Press, 1998. ISBN 1-57231-621-7. A good book with plenty of pragmatic ideas on how to make a project succeed. Its content ranges from engineering management hints to product and program management guidance.

Various authors. *Managing Product Life Cycles: From Start to Finish*. Cambridge, MA: Harvard Business School Press, 1992. ISBN 0-87584-277-1. A collection of articles from *Harvard Business Review*. Some articles are slightly dated, and not all articles are appropriate for software product life cycle management, but a few are nevertheless extremely useful. "The House of Quality," by John R. Hauser and Don Clausing, provides an interesting framework for team-oriented design, where marketing and engineering talk to each other.

About Dan Condon

Mr. Condon held software product and program management positions at firms such as Microsoft, NetIQ, Rendition Networks, and Avasta. His interests and experiences span a variety of areas, ranging from operating systems, systems software, user-interface systems, applications management software, and software provided as a service. His earlier experience includes software engineering positions at Digital Equipment Corporation and Xerox, where he worked on operating systems and systems software. He is a graduate of the University of California, Berkeley.

ASPATORE
C-Level Business Intelligence™